MY UNDERGROUND WAR

The True Story of How a Group of British Prisoners-of-War
Fought Back Against their Nazi Captors

By Albert Edward Clack

Edited by Albert John Clack

Copyright © 2014 by Albert John Clack

This book is dedicated to_all the brave British and other Allied soldiers who were incarcerated in Stalag VIIIB and other such prison camps; to the Soviet soldiers who liberated my father and many of his comrades; to the kind Polish civilians who looked after Dad and other escaped POWs; and to those German soldiers and civilians who, in spite of the dangers involved, struggled against the Nazi ideology.

The Lost Thirty Thousand

Hungry and weary and tired on their feet
Even the worst camp for sleep they would greet.
Thirsty and maddened at every stride
The spirit of hope they would never hide.

Mile after mile through the dust and the heat
Marched brave British hearts that would not be beat:
Taffies and Cockneys, Geordies and Jocks
Marching to Germany, some in their socks.

Jackbooted guards jeered as they went
Thirty more miles, with many backs bent.

How many died we will never know,
But to survive they just had to go
To Stalags or work in a mine, enslaved men.

Sapper Albert E. Clack

PROLOGUE

This is the story of five British soldiers, from different regions of our island nation, with different backgrounds and civilian occupations, from different regiments, thrown together as prisoners-of-war in a faraway land after being captured amid the chaotic defeat of the British Expeditionary Force in northern France at the end of May and beginning of June, 1940.

Throughout my nearly five years as a prisoner of the Germans during the Second World War, I was forced to work; initially, for a short period, building a road; and thereafter, as punishment for sabotage, in a coal mine in Gleiwitz, a town then in the south-eastern corner of Germany, and now called Gliwice, in Poland. The town lies on the western side of the heavy industrial conurbation centred on Katowice, in the region known as Upper Silesia. It was at Gleiwitz that Hitler had staged a fake Polish attack on a radio station on 31 August 1939 which served as a pretext for invading Poland the next day, precipitating the outbreak of war with Britain.

For most of us, the daily routine was filled with working, getting hold of enough to eat, and simply trying to survive; but we hated our captors, and some of us were determined to find ways of carrying on the war against them from within Germany.

I was born in 1920 in Brighton, the only son of Albert Henry Clack, an engine driver on the Southern Railway, and his wife, Daisy. I was unhappy at home, so when I was 18 years old, seeing that Europe was in crisis, I joined the Territorial Army. Thus, when war was declared on 3 September 1939, I was soon away from home and serving my country with pride and determination to play my part in defeating fascism, as a Sapper in the Royal Engineers.

Bill Burgess had been born near Durham. Most of his youth had been spent during the First World War and the economic depression of the 1920s. He had followed his father into working in the coal mines of County Durham; but this was not the way of life that Bill wanted, so he left the pits and finished up hanging around on street corners and getting into trouble with the law. Eventually he and some of his mates carried out what they thought was a successful robbery on a local shop. With money in his pocket, Bill was accosted by a prostitute in a pub and went to her room for the night. On awakening to find her going through his pockets and putting his money into her bag, he jumped out of bed, knocked her to the floor, dressed hurriedly and left with the proceeds of the robbery intact; but within hours the police had arrested him for the assault and linked him with the robbery. He was jailed, but released in October 1939 after serving only part of his sentence, on condition that he join the army. That was how Bill became a Private in the Durham Light Infantry.

Richard 'Smudger' Smith was the son of a farmer with a mixed farm in Kent. His father had hoped that by taking his son into farming he would save him from having to join the army if war broke out with Germany, as farming was a reserved occupation. However, Smudger didn't like the farming work, and when he was called up for the First Militia he did not apply for exemption.

Andrew 'Jock' McFarlane had been born in Glasgow. When he was about two years old his mother had died, and his father subsequently showed no wish to be responsible for him. At the age of nine he had become involved in a street fight because of some remarks about his mother. Being in possession of a dangerous knife, he was taken into care. As soon as he was old enough he had joined the Glasgow Highlanders.

The fifth member of the group was Charlie 'Chuck' Wilson. Details of this soldier's background are left out of this narrative for reasons which will become clear as the story unfolds.

At first we seemed to have little in common; but in the working party known as E22, we became close friends. That is to say, four of us did. About the fifth, we began to entertain sinister doubts regarding his loyalty.

PART ONE

DEFEAT AND CAPTIVITY

CHAPTER 1

For some weeks after it was announced that we were at war with Germany, my unit remained stationed at our depot in Brighton, and we continued to spend our nights at home. Then, at the beginning of October 1939, we were told we were moving to the West of England, and I was sent off as part of an advance party. As a field company of the Royal Engineers, we were going to be carrying out various field works, and our new station was to be near both open country and seaside. It turned out to be Bridport, Dorset; which was very lucky for me, because it is where I met a young woman called Edith Down, daughter of a Bridport tailor, with whom I fell in love, and who wrote to me, sent me parcels, and kept my spirits up throughout my long captivity; and who became my wife at St Peter's Church, Preston, Brighton, a few months after I returned to England in 1945. Most of my military training in that area was spent preparing for specialist tasks such as laying land-mines and climbing up cliffs from beaches. We also spent two weeks at Pangbourne, Berkshire, where we practised building and launching various types of bridge across the River Thames.

We sailed for France from Southampton on 2 April 1940 and landed at Cherbourg, where we were put on a train for a 10-hour journey to a small place called Saint Georges, where we were encamped in tents and in farm buildings. For a while we settled in there to a normal army routine, and the days passed quite pleasantly.

When we moved north-eastward again, approaching ever nearer to the enemy, it was to a very hospitable town called Bailleul, almost on the border with Belgium, where we stayed for about two weeks. Now, with our pre-war training and all that we had learnt since mobilisation, we thought we were as ready to meet the enemy as we should ever be.

I believe it was on about 8 May 1940 that we assembled to cross the border into Belgium; and it was only after we did so that we heard that the Germans had invaded Holland and Belgium. Advancing across Belgium, we were full of hopes that now we would be able to engage the Hun and drive him back to Berlin. How wrong could we have been? In fact, we simply moved from one position to another; whenever we were consolidated, we received orders to withdraw; and so it went on.

After almost 20 days we came back through Bailleul and took up a position on the side of a hill called Mont des Chats. The idea, we were told, was to give support to a company of infantry so that other troops who were coming that way would be able to withdraw. After being plastered by mortar fire and dive bombers for almost two days, we were ordered to withdraw ourselves. The other company of infantry had already gone, and troops whom we were supposed to be covering had, in fact, already passed through before we had arrived.

A general instruction was given to make our way north towards the French coast, where further orders would be given. There was no advice that the British forces were to be evacuated from France. However, we did feel that something had gone seriously wrong when the Section Sergeant told us: "Push off, it's every man for himself."

Taking the position of the sun as a guide, we began making our way northwards. A small group of us kept together, thinking there was safety in numbers. There was no officer, and the only NCO with us was responsible for pay and had little knowledge of map reading or fighting the enemy. He produced a map from his pack but couldn't read it, so he handed it to me. It was a school atlas printed in 1924. A few towns were marked, along with First World War battlefields. There were no details of roads. We were lost in a foreign country without maps, orders or officers, and we had no idea where our main forces were, nor where the enemy might be.

It was the latter whom we next encountered. Our first engagement of the war was with a few German soldiers who were resting in the corner of a field by a farm wagon. As soon as they recovered from their surprise at seeing us, they started shooting, but we had more firepower. We left all except one dead, and he was very badly wounded.

Moving on, we saw a cluster of houses ahead, and

hoped there might be some French civilians still there who could supply us with something to drink to wash down the food we were carrying in our haversacks. As we drew nearer, we saw that the houses were at a road junction. On our left was a field on which crops were growing and on our right a patch covered in weeds. Little did we realise that these were our last moments of freedom, and that we were walking into a trap which was to seal our fate for the next five years.

The first indication that we were in trouble was when a group of civilians appeared from the biggest house, first waving their arms in the air, then holding them high above their heads. In a moment we were surrounded by German soldiers. The position was obviously hopeless, so our NCO told us to surrender, and we threw down our rifles.

For the first time I heard myself being given orders by a German, and it got right up my nose. I had no idea that obeying the orders of German guards was now to be my life for almost five years, until the far-off winter of 1944-45, when Uncle Joe Stalin's gigantic, avenging Red Army would roll inexorably across Poland into Germany and finally liberate me and thousands of other British prisoners-of-war from our long nightmare of captivity and hard labour.

With an array of rifles pointing at us, we had no alternative but to obey. A German officer told us to line up along the roadside, where his soldiers searched us for hidden weapons. They took our bayonets, threw them against a wall, and broke them. Left with only the haversacks in which we had carried our gas masks, we were marched away from that fateful road junction towards an unknown destiny.

Although we felt very dejected, we tried to march with our heads held high, as though we were still marching with the British Army; but with German soldiers constantly jeering, it was difficult to keep up the bravado all the time.

What we had no inkling of while being herded away from our home country and towards Nazi Germany, was the chaotic nightmare taking place just a short distance away on the beaches at Dunkirk, and the heroic rescue by civilian boat owners of so many thousands of our comrades, cut off from land retreat by encircling German forces.

At long last we halted near a wall around a church and its graveyard. The town we had arrived in was Ypres: we had crossed the border from France into Belgium. We were searched again, and the Germans stole whatever valuables they found, such as watches and rings.

We were made to stand with our backs to the wall, and we could hardly fail to notice that it was already pockmarked with bullet-holes; so it looked as if we were going to be shot there and then. It was up against that church wall in Ypres that I learned the real meaning of fear: my mouth went completely dry, I was unable to swallow, and sweat ran down my face into the corner of my mouth.

For a while I thought my life was going to end outside that church. Little did I know that it was to be at another church, far, far away to the east, that my freedom was to be restored to me, 56 seemingly interminable months later, by the Russians.

There was, of course, no firing squad, otherwise I would not be writing this. Instead, the German officer who had captured us, and who had accompanied us thus far, told us with a swagger: "You are going to Berlin, but not in the way you had thought."

He was then joined by another German officer, who took us into the church, and told us we could sit down, and that we were going to spend the night there. The officer who had captured us declared: "Tommy, for you the war is over."

The arrogance of his words and the manner in which he spoke them put some steel back into my spirit, and I silently vowed to prove him wrong: that somehow I would ensure that for me the war would not be over, and that in some small way I would find opportunities to carry on the fight against the Nazis and their evil creed.

For the time being, I knew I was 'in the bag'; but at that moment, in that Belgian church, I promised myself that, if ever it should prove humanly possible, someone, somewhere, was going to pay for my liberty having been taken away.

Later in this story I shall tell how two very nasty pieces of work, both members of Hitler's Nazi Party, were indeed made to pay - with their lives.

CHAPTER 2

When one goes to prison for a crime against society, one usually knows the maximum length of the sentence. There is a release date to look forward to. There is hope. But we, as prisoners-of-war, were to be held for a period of indeterminate duration. We did not know how long the war would last. We did not know who would win. We did not know whether we would ever see our loved-ones and homes again. We did not know whether we would live to enjoy freedom again or die in captivity.

No transport was available to take us to Germany, so day after day we were marched toward the frontier. On the journey, food was only issued once, after we had been made to work on a transport depot abandoned by the French near Oudenaarde, a Belgian town about half-way between the French border and Brussels.

As we were being herded eastwards, I hoped I would eventually find other Tommies who had resolved after being captured that they would try by some means or other to carry on the war from within Germany; but if this were ever to happen, it must for the time being remain merely a speculation about a very uncertain future.

Gradually the number of British prisoners increased, and stories circulated about the military muddle that had occurred. The apparent truth was more outrageous than any of us could have dreamed up.

Many of the men fell sick en route: some with dysentery, some with ulcers on their legs and feet; but all carried on in the hope of eventually receiving medical attention.

We crossed from Belgium into Holland, and some of the Dutch people in Maastricht and Meersen tried to help us with food and medical attention; but the Germans pushed them aside and forced us to walk so fast through those towns that we were almost running. At last we crossed the border from Holland and entered the German town of Aachen.

One jeering guard told us that now we were going to

be put on the Berliner Express and taken to the heart of the fatherland. We were then loaded into cattle trucks without any facilities; and by the time we reached our destination, a small station which seemed to be in the middle of nowhere, the conditions were terrible. We had, in fact, arrived in the German town of Lamsdorf, now in Poland and called Lambinowice, the site of the vast prisoner-of-war camp known as Stalag VIIIB. The name will never be erased from my memory.

Now began a process that was to become routine during the coming years: lining up and being counted over and over again. We eventually wondered if they ever got their sums right. On this occasion, an officer with gold braid all over his uniform and cap walked up and down our lines at least six times before satisfying himself that no prisoners had joined or left the train en route.

We were ordered to fall in, in a column of four abreast, and marched through a gate into the camp, at which point we were counted again. Then in groups of 50 we were told to move towards some buildings which had a notice above the large double doors reading: 'Baden' (baths). Once inside we were hustled into stripping off all our clothes, and then shepherded along to have all our hair cut off using what looked like sheep-shearing tools. Once this operation was completed we were ordered to take a shower in an area scarcely large enough for the 50 of us. The so-called soap they gave us was useless and only rubbed the skin. It seemed to be made of some kind of abrasive such as pumice, and a bonding material. After about 15 minutes the water was turned off. Without towels, in an open-sided building like a barn, we dried ourselves in the heat of the sunny day and a gentle breeze. Our uniforms were returned to us smelling of some foul disinfectant. Once dry and dressed, at the main camp buildings we were photographed, documented and inspected by a medical officer who apparently spoke no English.

So the routine of the camp began. It was a matter of making sure we would survive. For two weeks we had eaten very little, so food became our main interest. There was a daily issue of a small bowl of soup and a small piece of black bread.

We began building up a new vocabulary of camp slang and German. A goon was a German guard. Appell was the word used by the goons to summon us for roll-call and counting at least three times a day. Chathouses were the latrines - a double meaning, because it was both where you could talk without being overheard, and where you went to 'chat out'; in other words, rid yourself of 'chats' or lice.

The standard reply to a German when he spoke was either "Deutschland kaput" or "propaganda". We nicknamed the official German interpreter 'South American Joe' because he had an American accent and told wild stories about having learned to speak English in America. It was apparently his job to come into the compound, talk in what seemed to be a sympathetic manner, and spread rumours.

One rumour that grew seemingly from something said by South American Joe was that we were to be moved nearer to Berlin so as to provide protection to the civilian population as 'human shields' against air raids. It turned out not to be true; but soon afterwards some of us were ordered to prepare our meagre belongings for a move, and we were sent to other, smaller camps, where we were put to work.

I was sent in a working party to Camp E43 at a village near some mountains between the towns of Frankenstein-in-Schlesien and Glatz, south of the city of Breslau. These are all now in Poland and called Ząbkowice Śląskie, Klodzko, and Wroclaw. Our job was to build a road through woodland to link up with a village about two miles away. We deliberately made a mess of it, and the area commandant told us we would be punished for sabotage. We did not know yet what form the punishment would take; still less, that it would last for the rest of the war. What we did know was that we had struck the first blow in our own, small war against the German war effort from inside the Third Reich. It was by no means to be the last.

On about 10 April 1941 we were transported to our punishment in a separate carriage attached to a passenger train. When it eventually stopped at the town of Gleiwitz we were ordered to fall in on the platform. Once again we were counted three times before the officer in charge was satisfied that no-one had escaped or joined the party.

We were marched out of the station and along a wide, fairly straight road. Before long we spotted the unmistakeable shapes of pit winding gear. There we were told to turn right, entering a yard attached to a coal mine. Again we were counted.

We were then met by the Senior British Officer, a Platoon Sergeant-Major from the Welsh Guards. He gave us a long lecture about discipline and warned us that he wanted no trouble between us and the German guards.

After the lecture, we were directed to our quarters and told we could draw rations, which turned out to be a bowl of vegetable stew and potatoes boiled in their jackets together with a loaf of black bread and a portion of margarine. The margarine was meant to last us for the rest of the week.

The next morning was occupied by a farcical pretence of a medical examination to certify that everyone was fit to work below ground. The whole party of 50 prisoners was passed as fit to work in the mine; even one of the older men who had ulcers all over his legs, and another man who was so weak from dysentery and constant bleeding that he had difficulty even walking to and from the medical centre.

I began working the following morning. We were awoken at 5.30am and ordered to be ready to enter the cage and ride down to the pit bottom at 6.30am.

At the pit office I was given another number and was told that this number would be used to draw my disc at the start of each shift to ensure that I was at work, and I would be paid for my work at the end of each month. If I did not draw my disc I would not be registered as working, a search would be made for me, and I would not be paid.

The mine was non-gas, therefore we did not have to use safety lamps. We worked with carbide lamps which produced an open flame.

The level we commenced working at was 365 metres below ground. We were met by the District Obersteiger (Senior Overseer) and he told us whom we were to work with and what the job was.

The rock in this area had at some time cracked and the coal seams did not run level, but at angles of at least 40 degrees. Those that were working on coal faces therefore had very little shovel work to do as it was cut out and ran in pans to a bunker and the wagons were filled at the bottom of the chute of the bunker. I was detailed to go with a hewer working in a section that had the job of cutting main roads from one coal seam to the next.

There was an unexpected advantage to this type of work: once down the pit, we had no German soldiers as guards, and they very rarely came inside the compound except to call out the various shifts for work. The daily routine continued, and if the Sunday was a rest day, the next week we changed shift.

The time that we were not working below ground was very much our own, and this enabled me to meet and talk with others who were at the camp. During rest-time conversations I met Bill Burgess, Richard 'Smudger' Smith, Andrew 'Jock' McFarlane and Charlie 'Chuck' Wilson. Each of us expressed the desire to carry on the war against Hitler from within the prison camp; although later it became clear that one of our number was insincere about this.

We determined in secret discussions that we must first get to know the terrain, both below and above ground. Also we needed to get to know the enemy better. We wanted to know which of the civilian workers were German, which were Poles, who could be trusted and who could not. Eventually we would discover that some of the Poles were already part of the underground anti-Nazi movement working in the area. What was amazing was just how many. But it took time, patience, and extreme discretion for this to become apparent. We also needed to work on our communication skills; breaking down the language barriers. Conversations below ground were held in a patois which mixed German and Polish. It took us time to learn it, but eventually we knew enough to be able to converse with the civilian miners. However, we were very careful about what we said to them; within our group there was a bond of secrecy; earlier attempts to escape having been thwarted by information being passed to the German guards.

It was not until the autumn of 1941 that my underground war could really get under way.

CHAPTER 3

At last we heard a whisper that 25 NCOs were planning an escape. We received approval by the Senior British Officer for us to help by creating a diversion. The timing was settled as the night of the last Thursday of October, 1941. In the meantime, Bill Burgess and I were working under a German ganger called Franz Muller. He was a lazy individual, so he allowed Bill and me to do the drilling of the rock face as well as the positioning of the explosives in the holes, leaving him with nothing to do but come back and detonate them.

On the night in question the drilling was completed at about 4.30am and we were given the box of shots to fuse and ordered to start charging the holes. Without using any extra shot, we loaded the holes to fire in the wrong order, with the intention of bringing down part of the tunnel roof and causing chaos. Franz went away, leaving us unsupervised, and did not come anywhere near the face until all was ready. He checked that the firing wires were correctly connected and trailed it back to the funkhole. He suspected nothing. When we were all in safe positions he depressed the handle on the charger. There was an almighty noise, and it was immediately obvious that something had gone seriously wrong. After the explosions, as the dust cleared, following normal procedure, we returned to the face. The roof had a hole in it large enough for a couple of buses. Rocks had been blown back down the tunnel and had damaged the compressed-air pipes. Further rock falls were still occurring, and another section of roof was caving in back along the tunnel. In short, the whole area was now unsafe. We tried to look innocent.

Franz was worried that the breaking-up of the rock would continue in the roof back to the point where it was reinforced by girders and overhead packing. We therefore all withdrew back to the main road leading to the shaft bottom, where he reported to the night duty overseer. Now began a lot of rushing around to get everyone out of the area, including other miners working in nearby tunnels. At the office at the assembly area at the shaft bottom a phone call was made to advise the guards back at our camp that we were coming up early. This was part of our plan, as we would normally have been escorted back by the same guards who brought in the day shift; but because of our early finish, four guards had to be sent from the barracks to collect us, and would have to wait for us to complete washing. The camp itself would be left with only four other German soldiers who were near the end of their night duty on the perimeter fences around the camp, and they would be tired.

With security thus weakened, the escaping British NCOs had little difficulty making their break from behind the latrines.

Their absence was not immediately discovered by the Germans. Those on parade for work at 2pm were counted several times, yet still the escapees were not missed. The prisoners on the afternoon shift, whom they should have been among, were taken to the pit as usual, and collected their discs. It was only when a check was then made on the discs that had not been collected that the Germans realised some men were missing.

The day shift now returned from the pit to the camp. The German Commandant entered the compound with six of the guards and everyone was ordered to parade. We were counted several times, and then he addressed us in German. Our own interpreter told us what he had said. The gist of it was that we had committed sabotage and that the men who had escaped would all soon be captured and no doubt shot.

Many weeks passed before we received any news, and when we did it was from the oldest of the guards; a man whom we called Twinkle-Toes, because he had had some toes on each foot removed. He told us that all of the escapees had been caught after three weeks. Some had got as far north as the outskirts of the German port of Danzig on the Baltic Sea, which is today the Polish port of Gdansk, while others had crossed the mountains into Czechoslovakia and been captured near Prague. We were told that the operation had kept untold numbers of German police and soldiers occupied for three weeks.

My underground war had well and truly begun.

CHAPTER 4

When one of the escapees had been captured, he had food on him saved from Red Cross parcels. We had been receiving an issue of one food parcel and 50 cigarettes each week from the International Red Cross. Thereafter, to prevent food from being saved up for any future escape attempt, the Camp Commandant ordered the tins we received to be punctured. This led to waste and food poisoning.

The Senior British Officer refused to intervene, so eventually the British interpreter did so. After that, parcels were issued one between four of us every other day. This kept the Jerries busy with more administrative work.

Early in November 1941, snow started to fall. It stayed on the ground for a long time, with fresh falls now and then.

Just before Christmas, while things were quiet and the work in the mine was going on much as usual, the Germans suddenly told us we should arrange a concert, as we were being given two days off work on Christmas Day and Boxing Day.

We were forbidden to sing the National Anthem; but we did anyway. Led by a soldier from the Rifle Brigade called Tom Arnold, we sang two verses of Land of Hope and Glory, and between them, we sang our National Anthem. Two guards were on duty directly outside of the hut where the concert was held. They either did not notice, or decided to ignore it.

The concert was a great success. With the help of one of the older guards, we had been able to buy some barrels of beer. It wasn't very strong, but it made our celebrations a little more festive.

Early in the New Year of 1942, personal parcels started to arrive from home. In the first parcel I received was some much-needed underclothing. I was still wearing pants and vests that I had been wearing the day I was captured, as well as a set that I had found when we had been clearing up that transport depot in Belgium. Although they had been carefully washed and repaired, I was beginning to wonder what would happen when they finally disintegrated into rags.

A few weeks later, other parcels started to arrive, mostly cigarettes and tobacco. Together with the cigarettes that came in the Red Cross parcels, the supply among four of us sharing our stock of cigarettes was fairly good.

Although the German guards and civilian workers in the mine had coupons for smokes, they were only enough for 12 cigarettes a week. With our bigger stock of cigarettes we were now at an advantage over the guards and the miners. Eventually some Germans were prepared to do us favours in exchange for the occasional cigarette.

Our work had been on extending a tunnel which was due to break through and meet a similar one being cut towards us from another working. At last the two tunnels met towards the end of March 1942. All that remained for us to do was some tidying up and making up the roof, ready for the fitters to come in and lay the last section of railway track and connect up the compressed air pipes into the new heading.

Thus it came about that on the first Monday in April 1942 we rode down to a new level, 550 metres below ground, to commence the job of cutting a new access road to run from a coal seam known as Schuckman, about eight metres wide, to a seam that had been named Schuckman Begleiter (Schuckman Companion) and was the widest seam in the area, at up to 30 metres wide.

Owing to a fault in the strata, the coal seams did not run horizontally but at an angle. This made cutting out the coal much easier and to some extent less hard work. With the very wide seam becoming available, greater quantities of coal could be extracted, with less labour and less physical effort.

The main tunnel from the shaft bottom to the point where we were to commence the new tunnel was about ten metres wide, and we were to continue the new road at the same width. This meant that from rock face to rock face across the width of the tunnel we were to cut out to about 11-1/2 metres wide. The height of the tunnel was to be three metres after the shoring-up had been done and the correct width made by building up walls with a sand and cement mixture filled in with fairly large rocks. The rocks would be selected from those cut from the face as it was driven forward.

Although work began slowly, after two weeks of continuous toil the tunnel had progressed some 15 metres; but then we struck an area of very wet sandstone which indicated an unstable rock formation. The overseer gave the ganger instructions that the line of the road was to be diverted, and he was to start cutting on a new heading to move to the right of the water. Soon we were clear of the water and unstable rock and the face was advancing at a rate of 4-1/2 metres per day.

Until this time, each gang on each shift working on the heading had consisted of a German ganger, two Polish workers and one British prisoner-of-war. However, Hitler had by now invaded Russia, and many of the Poles were being conscripted into the German army for the Russian front. So now the gangs comprised one German, two British prisoners, and either a Russian prisoner or a Ukrainian prisoner from a labour camp about three miles away.

When this alteration occurred, it meant that I had Smudger Smith working with me in the same gang. The Russian POW who had joined us, whose name was Ivan, was very slight in build. We became friendly with him as time went on.

Our German ganger, Franz Muller, was well-known as a Nazi Party member. He never did a stroke of work, but just sat back while the work was being done by the POWs, even to the drilling of the face and preparing of the shots for firing. We learned from Franz, who could speak reasonable English, that he had spent a couple of years working in Wales before 1938, in a coal mine near Wrexham. At the start of each shift he would taunt us with stories of the bombing of Britain, and after finding out what our home towns were, he came out with lurid tales about their destruction from the air.

Because of his taunts, but above all because of his cruel persecution of our frail Russian friend, Smudger and I decided that Franz Muller would have to be taught a lesson. We did not, at this stage, realise that it would the last lesson he ever learned.

The conditions of British prisoners-of-war in Germany were no picnic; but we were lucky when compared with the Russians. For instance, they got food only once a day, consisting of either a bowl of cabbage soup or a portion of very stale black bread and a piece of raw fat. We, on the other hand, could supplement our rations with food from Red Cross parcels, and this enabled us to carry some grub with us when we were working.

About half-way through the shift it was usual to stop work for a break of about ten minutes. During this time we would eat whatever food we had brought with us, which was known as our 'snap'. Over time we had furnished ourselves with enamel bottles in which to bring coffee and small tins for our food. Naturally, we shared it with Ivan. We also gave him cigarettes, even though it sometimes meant giving Franz one as well.

One day, after we had driven the face of the tunnel some 50 metres past the watery area, Smudger gave Ivan a cigarette to smoke well before the time of our break. Franz started to rave and shout. It turned out he had lost all his cigarette coupons in the pithead changing rooms.

By break time he had quietened down, but he muttered to himself whenever we spoke to Ivan. We conversed with Ivan in a mixture of rudimentary German and Russian that we had learned. Suddenly Muller leaped up off the box on which he was seated, grabbed Ivan by the belt, knocked his sandwich out of his hand and kicked over the mug of coffee we had given him. The half-cigarette that he had saved to smoke after his food was thrown into the wagon of rock that we had just filled. Ivan jumped to the side of the wagon to recover the smoke and as he did so Muller kicked him up the arse. If he had been fully clothed it might not have been so bad, but the Russians were not issued with clothes to wear down the pit, so they removed their uniform and either worked in just their boots, belt and helmet, or sometimes they had on a small pair of pants. Ivan was virtually naked and terribly vulnerable.

This was not the first occasion that Ivan had been kicked by Muller, but the climax came a few days later. We had just finished shovelling the debris from the previous shift's blasting when I handed a cigarette to Ivan and lit one for myself. Muller turned round from his position on the face where we were to start drilling and the first thing he noticed was the cigarette Ivan was smoking. He shouted something that at first I couldn't understand but as he jumped on Ivan I realised he meant, why hadn't I given him a cigarette before I gave one to a Russki. Poor little Ivan, only about 5 foot 2 inches tall, was on the floor being rolled in the debris and punched in the head and stomach. His face was soon a mass of blood and dust from the debris and he was held to the ground with his belt being twisted tightly round his middle.

Smudger and I moved to rescue Ivan, and Muller immediately let go of his belt and tried to stand him on his feet; but the vicious attack had taken all the strength out of him. Smudger and I stood there threatening Muller with our picks, and he tried to say he thought he had seen Ivan fall and had been trying to pick him up.

We left Muller to do the drilling while we took Ivan back to a point along the tunnel where there was fresh water. There we washed his face and gave him a sandwich and a cigarette. After the explosives had been fired, Muller said nothing more to us, so we left to help Ivan to the shaft bottom. It was obvious he would be in no condition to work the next day.

We had been working on the night shift for a week without a break, and according to the routine we would have Sunday free, after which the shifts would be changed.

Arriving back at the camp that morning, we both felt sick at the brutal beating of our little Russian workmate, so before we went to bed that morning we went for a walk around the camp parade ground. Smudger wanted to tell the rest of the Russians who worked in the level at which we were working, but I felt that this was a matter we could deal with ourselves. What we planned during that stroll would mean execution for both of us if we were found out, so we agreed to tell no-one; not even Bill or Jock.

To understand how our plan was to work, some of the details of the mine and its procedures need to be explained.

When anyone went on shift he had to collect his numbered disc. This was carried all the time down the mine, and when at the end of the shift you arrived at the bath house, they were thrown in a bin, from where they were subsequently collected for issue the next time you went to work. Most of the Jerry workers tied their discs to their lamps with a short piece of wire, while the POWs usually put theirs in their tobacco tins.

It was the job of the Saturday night shift to complete the work of concreting the walls ready for the first Monday shift to do their job of packing up above the girders to the roof of the tunnel. The concrete had to be poured into wooden shuttering along the sides of the rock wall, placed so as to keep the width of the tunnel constant. After the Saturday night shift, the Germans often stayed on during Sunday morning to do maintenance work on the heading.

On the Saturday morning as we came off shift, we heard from some other Russians, whose job was to make sure the wagons were cleaned out when they came back down the shaft from the surface, that Ivan had died the previous afternoon.

That night, when we arrived at the face, Muller ordered us to mix three wagons of concrete while he prepared the shuttering and selected the sandstone rocks to go into the wall with it. Without further ado, we went about our task of preparing the cement. When it was ready, we pushed the wagons to where Muller had constructed the shuttering. Muller stood to one side and told us to start filling in with the cement. Before one wagon was completely empty, I called out to Muller that more rocks were needed at my end. He moved towards me and had to pass between Smudger, the wagon and the shuttering. As soon as his back was turned and he was facing me, Smudger hit him across the back of the neck with the heavy stick we used for puddling the mixture. Before he hit the ground we caught his body, lifted it over the top of the shuttering, and dropped it into the wet cement. We swiftly filled in on top of him with the remaining concrete. We also buried his lamp and snap tin in the concrete, but not before we had taken his numbered disc from the lamp.

We felt that justice had been done. Now we had to get away with it or we were dead men ourselves.

It was near the end of the shift, so nobody else came near us. At the bath house, we tossed Muller's disc into the bin along with ours. Nobody noticed. We bathed, changed into our uniforms as if nothing had happened, and said nothing to anybody.

When we reported for duty on Monday, there was gossip around that Muller had failed to turn up for work. The Germans assumed that he had gone "blau on Montag" - their slang for going absent after a heavy weekend of drinking. Another ganger was put in charge of us, and Ivan was replaced by a Ukrainian from the labour camp.

There now followed something that did our nerves no good at all. The Overseer decided to stay with our gang for about half of the shift. For most of the time, he sat on the toolbox, leaning his back against the new shuttering - exactly at the spot where we had entombed Muller. Now and then he asked questions, trying to find out if Muller had said anything to us that might give a clue to his whereabouts.

After he left, the ganger asked the Ukrainian to help him with the drilling of the face, while Smudger and I finished clearing up the last of the rock blasted out by the previous shift. It was nearly time to clear up for the end of the shift, and we asked the ganger why we had not stopped for our break. To my surprise, the German he spoke was even worse than mine. He said he was Polish and had been sent to work at the pit from many miles away because he was a miner by occupation. Of course, we then plied him with a lot of questions. We learned that he now lived nearby in a camp very similar to ours but without guards, and he was able to go out. He was paid less than the Germans, and was only permitted to travel to his home town once each month at the weekend, and only if there was no weekend working. His name was Joseph but he said that everybody called him Seph. The main reason we hadn't had our normal break was that Seph had forgotten to bring his snap with him. We immediately stopped work and sat down sharing our snap with Seph and the Ukrainian, from whom we could not get a word.

While we smoked after having eaten, Seph told us that Muller had been heartily disliked even among his German workmates, who regarded his having gone missing from the pit as a blessing. It was widely thought that he had most likely gone off with some of his Nazi Party comrades who had volunteered to work among the troops behind the lines at the Russian Front. We later learned that this became the generally accepted reason for his disappearance.

I had killed my first Nazi in my underground war, and I had got away with it.

CHAPTER 5

The rest of the summer and autumn of 1942 saw nothing out of the ordinary. Work followed the usual pattern. We heard from the German guards and civilians that the U-boats were creating havoc with shipping. They claimed that food was so scarce in Britain that nearly everyone was on the verge of starvation. We replied that it could not be so if the Red Cross parcels were still being sent to us from home. Not only that: most of the Germans we came into contact with wanted to barter for some of the things in our parcels, so presumably all was not well in the Thousand-Year Reich.

The new tunnel on which we had been working had broken through and passed the very wide seam of coal called Schuckman Begleiter. Our gang was then moved to a new task: to join up the 550-metre level with the 720-metre level by driving a shaft from a point about two kilometres away from the main shaft bottom.

Before starting on this internal shaft, we were dispatched to work at 720 metres. The area was very wet, with water being pumped out at a rate of 2,000 gallons per shift. We had to go through the process of compression before descending, and decompression at the end. This took about 2-1/2 hours off our working time. The conditions were very bad, and because of the amount of water dripping from the roof, our open-flame lamps were no good. We were therefore issued with battery-powered lamps shaped something like a Davy safety lamp.

I was now becoming increasing unwell, with very bad boils under my arms and between my legs. Consequently I was allowed three days off to rest. When I went back to work, the gang had been changed. Smudger was still working under the Pole, Joseph, but I was put into a different group under a German ganger called Heinrich Schmidt. The other Britisher was Bill Burgess, one of our group, and the four-man gang was completed by a 16-year-old local Silesian boy.

By late February, 1943, the area at the 720-metre level where the shaft was to break through was ready. We were then moved back to the 550-metre level, and were put under the control of an overseer who spoke perfect English. He was always referred to as Herr Dieter. His first name was a mystery. Later we found out it was Winston, which was why he refused to let anyone use it.

Those who had already been working on the sinking of the shaft had reached a depth of about 70 metres. When the drills were working here, the air was filled with dust, mostly from sandstone. The Germans and Poles were issued with masks to prevent them from breathing the dust into their lungs, but the prisoners-of-war had to endure the choking atmosphere without masks.

At the start of our third shift in this area, one of the German civilians refused to go down into the dust because he had left his mask at the pithead. Bill and I immediately refused as well. The overseer raised his stick above his head and approached us threateningly. We stood our ground, even though we knew that this particular overseer was well-known for beating prisoners. He asked us why we were refusing to work in the shaft. We said that if it was right for the German to refuse to work in the dusty air because he had forgotten his mask, then it was right that we should also be issued with dust masks. Now the Obersteiger came to see what was happening. They both started beating us about the head and shoulders, and then took us back to the shaft bottom. They phoned the camp and sent us up to the surface. When we arrived at the top, guards were there to meet us. They booted us and hit us with their rifle-butts while they escorted us back to the bath-house, where we were made to change back into our uniforms, then taken to 'the bunker'; a small building containing two punishment cells. We were locked up to await the Camp Commandant's return from town.

Much later, it must have been about midnight, the lights were switched on and the officer in charge of the district as well as the officer in charge of our camp came in and ordered us out into the open yard, where a large spotlight shone straight into our faces so that we could not see who was in the dark area. One of the officers moved into the circle of light facing us and the first words he uttered were "Englischer

Schweinhund". After this we heard very little more as we were set upon by about six Germans, some in uniform and some in long black overcoats. We were knocked to the ground and kicked until we feigned unconsciousness. I remember being lifted and almost thrown back into the cell, where I eventually fell asleep.

It was barely light when I awoke. Several more hours passed before a guard came in and chucked us out. Three German officers whom we had never seen at the camp before bundled us into an army truck standing ready at the gates leading to the main road.

There had been rumours that, for refusing to do any job, prisoners could either be shot or sent to one of the concentration camps.

At last the lorry stopped and we were pulled from the back seats and told to march across the centre of a parade ground to a large building on the opposite side. We had apparently come to a large barracks where German soldiers were sent for punishment, like 'The Glasshouse' at Aldershot. Once inside we saw our British interpreter from the camp, John, all dressed up with his army cap and his boots polished as if he were on parade. I wondered why he was present, and how he had managed to get his uniform looking as good as new.

He approached us in the company of an officer of the SS and told us we were being charged with sabotage, refusing to work, and disobeying the orders of the German Reich. Neither Bill nor I commented on this, but asked if we could at least have a wash, and what else was happening. The SS officer replied that we could go in the company of our guards to wash our faces and hands, and that we were to be brought that morning before a military tribunal.

Separately we were taken to the cloakroom and allowed to wash and use the toilet. Then, after standing against a wall for what seemed hours, we were shepherded into the long room where the tribunal was to hear the case.

Seated at a long table draped with flags bearing swastikas were three officers dressed in uniforms covered with braiding and ornate lanyards. Their hats were in front of them on the table. To their right was a very small table behind which sat John, our interpreter. The SS officer who had given us permission to have a wash told us to stand to attention in front of the long table. Two guards stood at either side of us and a third behind us. We could hear his wheezy chest as he breathed. A junior officer stood up and read the charges from a piece of paper, and it was translated. Various people were brought before the tribunal and made statements, some of which we could understand, while others made no sense at all. People we had never seen before appeared and told the officers that we had always been troublemakers and ought to be shot.

After what seemed to be an endless stream of witnesses, we were questioned by the German prosecutor and the senior officer of the tribunal, through the interpreter, for about 20 minutes. Then two of the guards pushed us back out to the hallway and told us we could sit down.

Seated on a bench on the opposite side of the hallway was one of the overseers who had been present when we had refused to work in the dust. His face was very stern until a guard told us we couldn't smoke, and then he smirked. Nothing else was said until we were hauled unceremoniously back on to our feet and escorted back into the tribunal.

Everyone was told to stand. The most senior officer read from a paper in his hand. When he had finished, John translated. We had been found guilty of refusing to obey orders and prejudicing the output of the mine at a time when the Reich needed extra coal production. Our refusal was deemed to be sabotage. We were sentenced to 21 days' solitary confinement in the military prison at Sosnowitz, a town which is now in Poland and called Sosnowiec, a short distance north-east of Katowice. We were asked if we had anything to say, and whether we were sorry for the trouble we had caused.

I felt very sorry for Bill, who seemed absolutely dejected, but I spoke directly to the officer as best I could in the German that I had learned during my imprisonment. I said I wanted to appeal on behalf of both myself and Bill, directly and not through an interpreter. There was a lot of whispering at the table, after which I was informed that they agreed, but warned me the sentence could possibly be made longer.

The appeal was arranged for the following morning. Overnight we were kept in the cells in the barracks. That evening we were given a mug of coffee each and a very small portion of black bread smeared with some white fat, plus five pieces of toilet paper each. I was told that when we had eaten we would be escorted to the toilet and then taken back to the cell for the night.

The following morning we were taken back to face the tribunal once again. Firstly we were given a lecture on the care of prisoners-of-war and what they should do in return. Then I was told to explain to the tribunal why I thought we should not be imprisoned. I explained in German exactly what had happened and why we had refused to work in the dust, after a German civilian worker had already declined to do so. There was so much muttering that I lost track for a while of what was being said by the officers amongst themselves; but gradually, by concentrating, I understood what they were saying. It appeared that the fact that the civilian worker had been the first to refuse to work in the dust had not come out during the examination the previous day. Without letting me say any more, Bill and I were taken back to the cells, and again warned that smoking was forbidden in an army prison.

The wait seemed endless. We were now put in separate cells, so we could not converse with each other, as we had been able to the night before. Finally, when it was almost dusk, a key was turned in my cell door and a new guard came in and told me to follow him. At the end of the passage he told me to lead the way up the stairs to the top floor. At the top of the stairs was another long passage and at the end we stopped and he knocked on the door. A voice from inside told him to open it, which he did, pushing me inside and closing the door behind me without coming in himself, which surprised me.

Seated at a large, heavy, wooden desk was the officer who had been in charge of the tribunal, and even more surprisingly he rose as I stepped forward. In perfect English he asked me where I had learned to speak German and said I had impressed the officers with my knowledge of the language and of the terms use in the mine. I replied that I had studied

German at the local technical college in Brighton, but the rest I had learned from working with civilians in the mine.

He then surprised me even more by moving to the side of the desk and sitting on the corner of it with his hands in his trouser pockets. I don't think I had ever seen a German officer with his hands in his pockets before.

"You may smoke if you wish," he said. I needed no more bidding and was soon lighting one of the Martins cigarettes I still had in my pocket. He then took my cigarette from me and told me to light another for myself as he was going to smoke the one I had already lit.

He said they had considered the case and the manner in which I had stated our defence. He thanked me for the information I had given them concerning the civilian worker who had refused to enter the shaft because he had forgotten his dust mask.

The miners, he said, had been given a bonus to ensure that they produced more coal for the war effort, and if they were neglectful and sabotaged the combined effort of others they had to be punished. This did not mean that as prisoners-of-war we could also sabotage the efforts towards more production, so we must be punished as well.

Here it comes, I thought, Bill and I are going down for a longer sentence. Why didn't I keep my mouth shut?

However, he went on, "Your punishment will not be as harsh as you expected, but the law is the law, and you will go to the military prison for three days and be kept in solitary confinement for these three days."

That was a lot better than three weeks, and infinitely better than being shot or sent to a concentration camp. I started to speak, but he interrupted and told me not to say anything, but listen.

"My rank is Major of the SS and my home is in Warnemuende near Rostock," he said. (Rostock is a north German port on the Baltic Sea coast). "There I learned English and engineering. When I was 18 years old I was sent to England to work and to learn how to make electrical control switches. Until March 1939 I worked at various factories and one was in your home town of Brighton, but alas, as the war was coming, I had to return and my father saw to it that I joined the SS."

After I had been told the outcome of the trial, smoked another cigarette, and even drunk a cup of coffee with the SS Major, I had still not learned his name. The interview had been most unusual and it stuck in my mind. There were so many things about it that were completely wrong: his manner, the way he spoke to me, and the fact that I had been left in the room with him without a guard.

There was a knock at the door. The Major sat back behind his desk, told me to stand correctly in front of him, and put the coffee cups out of sight. Only then did he call out, "Come in." The man who entered was a very old German soldier who looked as though he could have fought in the Franco-Prussian War. He asked if the prisoner was ready. The Major told him he could take me with him, but to be careful, as I was dangerous.

I was joined in the army lorry by Bill, who looked very dejected. As soon as we started to speak, the old soldier told us to hold our tongues, so we did so to please the old boy.

After driving for about an hour, the lorry stopped, sharp orders were shouted outside, and we heard heavy gates being opened and closed. The lorry trundled across what sounded like loose gravel, and then stopped. The canvas at the rear was opened, the tailboard was dropped, the two guards riding with us pushed us out, and we fell on the ground in front of two very much younger Germans dressed in uniforms a bit too big for them. They looked about 15 years old. I took at least two hefty kicks in the small of the back before I was on my feet. Helped by their rifle butts, we were marched in to see the officer in charge of the prison, who took some papers from the old man.

He read from these papers and then turned to me and asked, "Who is Kriegegefangenir (Prisoner-of-War) Number 13740." I told him I was, and he told me to call him sir. Our personal belongings were taken away and put in a box. He told me that Major Steiner (so that was his name) had given instructions for us to have facilities to take a shower. After showering, we were taken to separate cells.

My prison cell contained a bed made from three boards nailed together and held off the floor by two hinges on the wall side and a chain on the other, hanging from an eyelet in the wall about two metres above the floor; plus a stool. There was one very dirty blanket and a rolled-up piece of sacking which I would use as a pillow. In a corner was a wooden cubicle, which contained my toilet facilities. My boot laces, trouser braces and tie were confiscated, and then I was left alone. The light was left on, and I felt as if I were being watched, though I could see no-one.

I had heard stories of people who were held in this type of prison being woken up for further interrogation every time they nodded off to sleep. I must have been very tired, for suddenly I was aware of the sun shining in through a small, high-up barred window. The electric light had been turned off. I stirred and realised that I had been allowed to sleep all night and there had been no questioning. I went and used the toilet facilities. This consisted solely of a large metal pan on the wall with a pipe leading out through the wall. There was nowhere to wash. When I came out of the toilet cubicle I found a reddish brown bowl on the floor containing cold coffee and a piece of very hard, dry bread. This was to happen each morning. Solitary was to mean just that.

I guessed that the ration of coffee and bread would have to last me the 24 hours, and so took care not to drink all the coffee, although I was so thirsty that I longed to do so. I spent the first day sitting on the stool, on the edge of the bed, walking up and down, and thinking. With nothing to occupy my mind, it was amazing how long the day seemed to be. As the light began to fail, I sat on the bed, ate the last of my bread and drank the remains of the coffee. I stretched out on the bed, contemplated the ceiling, and endeavoured to recall some of the stories that I had read back home and re-examine their plots. This made the time pass much more quickly.

On the second morning, the coffee and bread were again left on the floor near the door while I was using the toilet. Now I decided my time must be used constructively. I sat facing the wall behind the bed with my back to the door. Every now and then I had the feeling I was being watched from the doorway. In my imagination I visualised a line of bricks across the wall as if they were a map of the main tunnel leading from the shaft of the mine to the various districts. I tried to remember points along that tunnel that were vulnerable, and at last I recalled one particular spot. By concentrating, I remembered the layout of the first junction on the main tunnel, which had a turn-off to the first district from which came the bulk of the coal being produced at that time. About half a kilometre from the shaft area there was a tunnel turning off to the left. The points on the rails were just short of the junction. Overhead the electric cable also separated and led into the district workings. This was the first point on the 550-metre level where the various services were split to provide the whole of the level with compressed air, electricity, water power, as well as large ventilators to draw out bad air.

What I had in mind was creating some kind of diversion so that the services at this point could be sabotaged. The working would then have to come to a standstill until everything was put back in order. If Hitler had ordered that the mines must produce more coal, it was our duty to ensure that they produced less. The Nazis had given me three days of peace and quiet in which to plan the next operation in my underground war. On that middle day, staring at the pattern of bricks and visualising the layout of the mine, the germ of an idea came to me. It would need the help of others to put into effect. I hoped that when we had served our short sentence we would be returned to the mine, so that we could develop a plan.

On the third morning, I awoke to find a guard sitting in the doorway of the cell. He ordered me to roll up the blanket and use the toilet, as the Prison Commandant wanted to see the two Englanders from the coal mine. Dirty, unshaven and in clothes that had not been taken off for about a week, I was ushered along in front of the guard to an office near where we had entered the prison. Six German soldiers were seated at desks; some were using typewriters, some writing in large books, and one was at a telephone switchboard. My belongings, including my braces and bootlaces, were returned to me, and the guard told me to dress myself properly. I was pleased to do so, as the boots without laces were uncomfortable, and my trousers were slipping down. Soon after I had laced up my boots and tied up my uniform, I was pleased to see Bill come in.

When we were both ready, the junior officer in charge of the office ordered us to stand to attention facing the wall. We were kept standing in this position for about half an hour, with an occasional prod from a rifle. Then we were sent into the Prison Commandant's office. He was sitting behind a desk with two large pictures behind him, one of Hitler, the other of Heinrich Himmler, the head of the SS. In a very quiet voice he asked us if all our belongings had been returned. I told him my cigarettes in a round tin had not been returned, and Bill told him his cigarettes had also been kept. The Commandant shouted at one of the guards and told him to find out what had happened to them. After a short wait, the German guard who had confiscated our things on arrival appeared and said they had been smoked by the Jungvolk soldaten. This was a reference to the Deutsches Jungvolk, an organisation in Nazi Germany for boys aged 10 to 14, some of whom became child soldiers. These were the boys who had met us off the lorry and kicked us while we were on the ground.

It seemed we would not get the cigarettes back, but speaking in faltering English the Commandant said the boys would be punished, and possibly sent to the Russian Front.

There followed a lecture on how we must do as we were told and obey orders, in which case we would not be punished again. Then he told us the war was going well for the Germans and that soon they would be in London and the storm troops would be marching down The Mall.

All this was leading up an offer: if we wished, we could be on the winning side, as we were being given a chance to join the British Free Corps. This was a unit of the Waffen SS recruited from among British and Dominion prisoners-of-war. (Editor's note: Only a handful of men ever joined). He showed us photographs of what he said were Britishers wearing the Free Corps uniform, sitting in front of a café, drinking from large beer mugs and smoking cigars.

Bill scrutinised the photo, turned to me and said,

"There's Charlie Wilson from our camp." I looked at the picture again, and I felt sure Bill was right.

The Commandant argued that soon all British prisoners would be joining, and suggested we join now and become NCOs before the others volunteered. When we refused, his friendly manner disappeared, and he ordered the guards to take us away and send us back to our camp. Waiting in the guardroom adjacent to the prison gates, we were allowed to sit down, and an older German brought us a mug of coffee and rolled us a cigarette from some tobacco he had in his pouch.

At about midday a lorry arrived outside, and we were loaded on board. By the time we arrived back at the camp, we were very hungry. We had been on coffee, bread and water for three days, and immediately before that, virtually nothing for three days. Luckily we arrived too late to join our normal shift, so we did not have to work that day. We cleaned up, collected a Red Cross food parcel, and prepared something to eat. The first cup of tea was like nectar; the first corned beef and beans tasted nothing short of dining at the Ritz.

I suddenly realised that my 23rd birthday had been spent in prison. In a melancholy mood, I wondered when I would next be able to celebrate a birthday at home. Soon, however, dramatic developments in the pursuit of my underground war were to chase such thoughts from my mind.

CHAPTER 6

Two things were uppermost in my mind as we settled back into camp life. One was the question of whether Charlie Wilson really was a member of the German Free Corps. The other was the plan that I had dreamed up in my prison cell to disrupt output from the 550-metre level.

That night, when Jock came in from work, Bill and I discussed it with him. It was a part of the working that Jock knew well, because he rode there every day with a locomotive driver. We also brought Smudger in on the plan.

Where the rails turned off from District One, the overhead wire hung slightly lower at a point where it also had a junction. Within a foot of the wire were the compressed air pipe and the telephone cable, both of which led to the districts further in from the shaft, and to the level between 550 metres and 365 metres, where the air returned from the furthest point. A pipe carrying water from the working back to the shaft was also nearby. We wondered whether it would be possible to tamper with the roof of the shaft in such a way that, when a locomotive pulling a train load of coal to the shaft passed, it would trigger off an apparently accidental collapse, thus disrupting all those services and putting a section of the mine temporarily out of action.

We decided not to inform the Senior British Officer. The fewer people who knew what we had in mind, the less chance there was of a leak. Besides, he might not agree to it. In addition, Smudger felt that Bill and I ought to keep out of it, as the Germans were keeping us under surveillance as potential troublemakers because of our recent court martial.

Months went by, and we were becoming a little despondent, as we had found no way of putting our plan into operation. Bill and I were no longer working in the same gang. He was sent to work on a coal face in one of the worst sections of the mine. They had to stand in about six inches of water and do most of the cutting with pickaxes.

I was put under a ganger called Erich, whose father was a winder at the main shaft. Our job was enlarging the main tunnel on the farthest side of District 5 so that it could be cut through to another working in a pit adjacent to ours. We were cutting through sandstone most of the time, and the air was full of dust when we were drilling. Although we had been issued with masks since my refusal to work in the shaft without one, the air here became so bad sometimes that the masks became clogged with dust so that it was impossible to breathe through them.

One day, shortly before Christmas of 1943, after coming off shift, I had great difficulty in breathing, was coughing badly, and bringing up some blood. That night I reported to the British Medical Officer, known affectionately as the Mad Major because of his skill in carrying out operations with a razor blade. He was concerned, and the German officer in charge of the camp gave him permission to take me to hospital. The next day at 9am the Mad Major came for me, and together with a guard we went to the local railway station and boarded a train for the nearby town of Hindenberg, which is now in Poland and called Zabrze. There I was subjected to various tests, including X-rays, and after consultations with the British Medical Officer it was agreed that I had a coating of stone dust on my lungs and should no longer work in a dusty atmosphere. As things eventually turned out, I was to spend the rest of my life suffering from pneumoconiosis, often known as the miners' disease.

Back at the camp, the German Officer in Charge held a meeting with the MO, a Red Cross official, the mine Obersteiger, and me. On the recommendation of the hospital doctors and the Red Cross official, I was given the option of coming out of the mine and working out-of-doors in the timber yard. However, the Red Cross official, who was Swedish, advised me that I might be better off working below ground, as I would be less likely to catch cold, which would make my lungs even worse. The Obersteiger said I could be found a job with one of the locomotive drivers. Until then, I was given three days' sick leave.

I wondered why they had been so considerate. The Red Cross officer told me later it was because they were supposed to ensure that prisoners-of-war were protected from industrial diseases, and had been seen to have failed to take adequate precautions. I believe it was also because of the presence of the Red Cross officer that I got three days off work.

The next day in the barrack room Jock told us he had a plan. It would become possible when the locomotive driver with whom he was working began giving him instruction when they were taking timber into the districts on a night shift. This was set to begin after Christmas. Timber was taken into the various districts during night shifts so as not to interfere with the movement of coal wagons during the day and afternoon shifts. The plan involved exploiting the German driver's laziness, so that it would look like his negligence rather than sabotage by a British prisoner.

After a rest day at Christmas, there was a changeover of shifts. Jock went on to night shifts and I was on mornings. I was now working with a German called Joseph, who had been a miner all his working life. Ever since an accident in the pit had crushed his left foot, he had walked with a severe limp. He was then made a locomotive driver. When I went to work with him as his assistant, he took the opportunity to teach me to drive, so that he could spend most of the shift sitting in the conductor's seat. I was happy to drive, because it accustomed the other German workers to seeing me enter areas that prisoners were not supposed to enter.

One Friday, when Jock was getting ready for the night shift, and I was preparing the cooking from our Red Cross parcel, Bill mentioned the matter of Charlie Wilson and the photograph we had been shown at the military prison. I asked whether it were possible that we had been mistaken. Jock mentioned that some weeks before, while Bill and I were at the court martial, two prisoners from our camp had been called out by the Germans and then packed their gear, telling everyone they were being moved to a camp near Berlin for a rest from work. On the same day as we had arrived back from Sosnowitz, they had returned looking very well, almost as if they had been on holiday. Previously these two had had very little to do with one another, but now they seemed to be friends and shared everything. One was Charlie Wilson; the other was Irish and was known as Paddy. We agreed to have a private talk with our Medical Officer; whom we regarded as the Senior British Officer, and not the NCO who had assumed the position. This was to be done on the Sunday morning, when Bill and I would attend the sick parade.

Meanwhile, it was agreed that Jock would put into action the plan that he had explained to disrupt production that night.

It is worth mentioning at this point that some three months earlier a radio had been built by two of the boys in our barrack room, using items stolen from the pit, such as earphones from the telephones in the mine and electrical components from the shaft bottom storeroom. It had been assembled at night-time, the components hidden in small tins, with sheets of masking above them covered in margarine or jam. The connections were at the bottoms of the tins, and while standing in our lockers they looked no different from any other tins. It was the duty of each in turn to listen in to the radio, which was tuned to a signal beamed from the BBC to that part of Europe. However, Charlie Wilson was not let into this secret.

On that particular Friday night it was my turn to listen to the radio, and I was just listening to a programme about the events of the war when the pithead siren started to wail. We looked out of the windows towards the pit top. The winding gear and the unloading platforms were bathed in floodlights in contravention of the blackout regulations, so we knew that something must have gone wrong below ground. Bill and I hoped it was because of the action that Jock had been planning, but the siren and the lights prompted fears that there might have been an explosion. Time passed, and then our lads who were on the night shift arrived back in the camp early, and we were told that no-one would be called for the day shift.

Shortly before dawn, Jock came across to the locker beside our beds, said simply, "It worked," climbed on to the top bunk and settled down to sleep.

In the morning, breakfast consisted of a good old English cup of tea and biscuits, plus butter and marmalade from the Red Cross parcels; and everyone was cheerful knowing we had a Saturday without work, and that there was a possibility of Sunday also being free.

Bill and I went for a walk around the parade ground perimeter with Jock, anxious to know what had happened. He explained that the trainload of timber and other materials had been standing ready when they arrived at the assembly area at the bottom of the shaft. He had had to wait until his driver, a lazy German called Paul, appeared; then they moved off, soon after the face workers had left, riding in empty wagons to their various districts.

A lot of the timber was over five metres long, for use as top bars for shoring up the roof in the tunnel of District One, where they were cutting out on a wider stretch than before. When they arrived at the turn-off for this district, the locomotive was uncoupled from the first wagon, proceeded up to the next set of points, reversed on to the down line, and came back to stand alongside the timber wagons. The points were set for the wagons to go into the tunnel leading to the district, and the wagons uncoupled as far back as they were consigned for this part of the district. At this point Jock told Paul that he would show him a way to save time and effort. He suggested that he take a pole from one of the wagons, about 1.5 metres long. This was to be used as a shunt pole; one end placed against the front corner of the locomotive that was nearest to the wagons, the other end against the buffer bar of the last wagon to be pushed. Slowly at first, Paul started to shunt the wagons forward using the locomotive with the pole, and as they moved he became over-confident, just as Jock had hoped, and increased his speed. Then it happened. Where the timber overhung, the wagons started to wobble, then they were pushed together, and two of them angled up towards the roof, where they hit the overhead wire. There was an almighty electrical flash, the cable burned through, and a loose end whipped about, hitting the walls of the tunnel and the compressed air piping. Now the roof started to fall, bringing the ventilator trunking and the water pipes crashing down. The overhead cable fault registered back at the control room at the bottom of the shaft. This brought the duty overseer to the scene.

When he saw the damage, he blew his top. He told Paul he would be sent to a concentration camp. News gradually came through of havoc created further away in the other districts. The break in the compressed air pipeline meant they were unable to use their drills, and the fracture in the return water pipe caused the water level to build up in the worst wet areas. With the ventilators not working, the air soon became unbreathable at the coal faces. Everyone was ordered back to the shaft bottom and then up to the surface, and the overseer sounded the alarm siren.

We plied Jock with all sorts of questions. How bad was it? How long would it take to be repaired? However, because he had not been allowed to stay there, he could only tell us that there was considerable damage in that part of the main tunnel.

Whatever the extent of the damage should eventually turn out to be, another blow had been struck against the Nazi war machine; but we must never let them find out that the cause had been anything other than negligence by a German locomotive driver.

CHAPTER 7

As there had been so much excitement concerning the disruption of work at the 550-metre level, we had forgotten for a while that it had been our intention to mention our concern about Charlie Wilson to the MO on the Sunday.

However, an opportunity presented itself when Smudger cut his hand opening a tin of dried milk. I accompanied him to the sick bay, where the Major cleaned and stitched the cut. While he was working, I asked him about the Free Corps, and he said he had heard of it and had been told that a number of prisoners had volunteered, but mostly from other countries. When I explained my suspicions concerning Wilson, his only reply was, "Well, you could expect anything from him." He suggested we test him out.

Smudger and Jock had not seen the photograph and were a little worried that we could be mistaken, but they agreed that we should try to confirm our fears, and if we proved to be wrong, so much the better.

Several months now passed uneventfully in the camp. Then, on the night of 6 June 1944, Smudger and I were on radio listening duty and heard the report of the D-Day landings. A number of others were still awake and the news was soon passed round. In the morning the news was all around the camp, but nothing was said about how we had heard it. As we went on shift, I rode in the cage standing beside Charlie Wilson, and he asked me if I had heard about the invasion. "Of course," I replied, "everyone has." He said it was propaganda, but that even if it were true he expected the allies would soon be routed as we had been in 1940.

The drain on Jerry's armed forces was soon noticeable, as the more able-bodied guards were replaced by a new type of soldier. These were the Volkssturm, a people's militia set up during the latter months of the war by the increasingly desperate Nazi regime. They were mostly old men, dressed in civilian clothes, with either an arm-band or a single item of uniform. Twinkle-Toes remained with us, as did a little German soldier who was blind in one eye. Both were ready to trade favours with prisoners for cigarettes, chocolate and soap.

The vigilance of the new guards was very slack, so at last we thought we might be able to catch Charlie Wilson out. A new camp had been set up next to ours, housing female workers brought from the Ukraine. The word was put around for Wilson to hear that Twinkle-Toes was prepared to take some of us across the timber yard for a party in the female camp. Twinkle-Toes, the rumour said, would meet anyone who wanted to go at the rear of the latrines, and the fee was a bar of soap. It was known that both Paddy and Charlie had more soap than anyone else in the camp.

Lo and behold, they both turned up behind the latrines waiting in vain for Twinkle-Toes; but they had brought with them, hiding in the shadows, one of the new guards, dressed in a dark blue overcoat.

We gave this information to the Major, who agreed that we seemed to have two 'plants' in the camp. He called together some NCOs, and they agreed that a close watch should be kept on them, and that they were to be treated as outcasts. Some of the prisoners wanted to take more positive action against them, but we knew this would bring down reprisals by the Germans against all of us.

And so summer again became winter, and a fourth Christmas was passed in captivity. In the outside world, the Third Reich was being forced to retreat on all fronts, and its defeat now seemed only a matter of time. Then 1944 became 1945, and soon the progress of the war was to change our own lives in a very big way.

But before that, there is a terribly sad episode which must not go unreported; made even more poignant by its timing.

As I have mentioned, when we returned from our spell in prison, Bill Burgess had been put to work on a coal face where the working conditions were extremely bad. It was very wet, there were frequent roof falls, and the shoring-up was breaking, leaving very little headroom. Late on the afternoon shift of Wednesday 17 January 1945, the roof had been falling and new timbers were being erected to try to prevent a complete collapse. The new timbers seemed to be holding when there was a loud crack and the roof came down. Bill, his German ganger and a Russian prisoner-of-war were trapped on the wrong side of the fall. The noise of the fall alerted those nearby, but when they arrived they were unable to help. Someone made a telephone call back to the overseer's office at the shaft bottom, and a rescue team was soon on the spot. At about that time, the night shift was riding down to the pit, and we heard the news while we were being told our duties for the night. I was dispatched to the scene of the accident with my locomotive driver and two others, and we set about helping the rescue team clear the coal brought down by the fall. Many hours passed before we broke through. The only person we found alive was the German ganger, but even he was pinned between two heavy timbers and his chest appeared to be crushed. The bodies of Bill and the Russian were brought out, and the injured German was taken to the shaft and up to the surface. Bill had missed the end of our sojourn in the mine by five days.

At the spot where the fall had occurred, it was found that the air was foul, and this had been caused by fire breaking out in the coal face. This was the first fire I had experienced in the mine. Teams of workers, including POWs, were sent to extinguish the blaze.

As soon as the fire was under control, on Saturday 20 January, work was begun on closing down that working and building a fire-resistant dam. Jock and I were part of the teams detailed for the work. Jock's team on the day shift included a Polish fire officer who came originally from Krakow and had no love for the Germans.

I was on the afternoon shift. We were told the area must be closed off within 72 hours of the damping-down of the fire having been completed, which meant it had to be completed by the afternoon shift of Monday 22 January at the latest. On that Saturday, we still had no idea what a momentous day that Monday was to be in our lives.

I now found myself working with Smudger, as well as a Geordie nicknamed Rusty and a Ukrainian, under a German ganger called Heinz whom we all hated, because he was forever beating the Russians who worked under him, and he stole cigarettes from British prisoners. We were soon to make him pay for his cruelty, in what was to be the last deadly blow in my underground war.

The process of closing the face involved coating it with a wet mixture of lime and sand back to the point at which the dam was to be built. When the dam was complete, a watery mixture of lime and sand would be pumped in through pipes until the space was full of the mixture.

Our first shift was hard work, in foul air, with no break, and we all emerged with headaches. When we left the site on the Saturday night the dam had just been started. It looked as if three more shifts would be needed to complete the shutdown.

During January 1945, the will to work seemed to be slipping away from the Germans. Now, at the same time as we were closing down the burning coal-face while we were underground, a new sound had begun to make itself heard while we were on the surface: the dull rumble of distant artillery. The Russians were coming; and the sound of their guns ignited a glimmer of hope in the hearts of us POWs.

A rumour ran through the camp that the Soviet Army was only about 60 miles away and constantly advancing. Then on Sunday another rumour was heard: that the camp was to be evacuated the next day, and that we would be force-marched westwards, away from the approaching Red Army and deeper into Germany; which, although it would take us away from the Russians, would take us closer to the advancing allied forces.

That rumour became reality with incredible suddenness. The Senior British Officer ordered us to pack everything that we wanted to keep, and be prepared to move at any time.

The excitement in the camp was terrific. We felt we might at last be on our way home. We each packed as much as we could carry. I had just finished bundling up my pack when we were summoned to go to work. Amazingly, I realised it was probably the last time I would ever have to go down into that stinking mine.

Travelling into the area where we were building the dam, we asked the Germans and other civilian workers what was going on in the outside world, and it seemed from their replies that the Red Army was even closer than we thought. Now we hoped they wouldn't arrive while we were still down the pit, for we looked no different from the Germans in our pit clothes.

All that remained to complete the dam was filling the last hole in it, which was about a metre square, and then connecting the hoses to the pipes so that the lime mixture could be pumped in. The heavy blocks of soaked timber with which to brick up the gap were ready at hand, and Heinz climbed through the hole so that he was on the inside and we could pass him a bucket of lime mixture to coat the hole around the pipe so that the mixture would not escape when pumping began. While he was on the wrong side of the dam we continued filling in the hole until it was just large enough for him to climb back out through. At this point, the overseer came along, and we stopped work and stepped aside to give him space to survey how much was left to complete. When he saw that it was nearly finished, he ordered us to start pumping in the mixture before we finished shift. The night shift would then merely have to keep topping up the hopper from which the mixture was drawn. This gave us our chance to deal with Heinz.

We looked at each other. We whispered. We were thinking: since Heinz had been such a swine to all POWs, why shouldn't we see to it that this was his last job? We all agreed: Smudger, Rusty, the Ukrainian and me. So when Heinz poked his head through the hole to climb out, the Ukrainian hit him on the head with a pickaxe. It went through his helmet straight into his skull. He fell back into the sealed-off section of tunnel, and we pushed him down into the sludge of lime and sand. Swiftly we fitted the last few blocks into position, closing the hole, and covered the face of the dam with fireproof coating.

Four wagons of the lime mixture were standing ready, so we connected the hoses to the pipes going through the dam, and during the following hours the mixture was pumped in.

None of us said a word during the rest of the time we were working. When the next shift turned up, the engineer told them to carry on refilling the wagons so that the blocked-off section would be full by the morning. Mercifully, no-one seemed to notice that Heinz was missing.

On the last day in that mine, we had accounted for one more of the enemy. Overall, during our captivity, we had caused quite a bit of trouble to the Nazi war effort. For this group of Tommies, the war had by no means ended in 1940.

When we arrived at the pit-top we could see bright flashes in the sky, and the sound of the big guns had now become thunderous.

Late on Monday we were paraded and marched out of that camp where a number of our comrades had died, and many others had become victims of sickness from which they might never recover.

My underground war was over. My convoluted journey home was about to begin.

PART TWO

ESCAPE AND LIBERATION

CHAPTER 8

For some days the rumble of guns had been heard in the distance, and gradually the sounds had been getting nearer. We knew from the news heard on our radio that the Soviet Army was advancing over a broad front across Poland. On the night of Friday 19 January 1945, when we came up from the mine at about midnight, bright flashes lit up the edge of the sky on the far horizon to the east. They seemed very near because the whole area was covered in snow, which reflected the light.

For nearly five years we had been hidden from the world. Now the war was coming to find us.

Prisoner of War Camp E22 was abuzz with news the following morning that we were soon to be on the move. Then on Sunday the Senior British Officer told everyone to make up a pack of their personal belongings and to make sure they carried as much food from the Red Cross parcels as they could.

Stocks of food in our lockers were fairly low because of the German Commandant's rule that tins were to be punctured. However, adjacent to the German guardroom was a building containing a stock of parcels that had not been issued; so as dusk fell in the afternoon, a party went to cut the wire and make a hole in the plaster wall backing on to the camp. Security was slack, as the guards were themselves preparing to move, so we had no trouble in moving most of the parcels into the camp and stocking up our hastily prepared packs.

There was a grand smell of cooking in each barrack room that night as tins that had already been opened were converted into meals.

On Monday morning no guards entered the camp to call us out to work, and cooking was the order of the day. Some strange meals were prepared for breakfast.

At about midday, the Camp Commander held a parade without the usual counting and recounting, and informed us through the interpreter that the camp was to be evacuated later that day.

The rest of the day seemed to drag by, and when evening came and we had not been given orders to parade ready to move off, we made another raid on the parcel store, and another a great cook-up got under way throughout the camp. The radio was taken out of hiding and we took turns to listen in on the headphones. News of the Russian advance in the east and the Allied advance in the west gave us hope.

Most of us had suffered from hunger on the long march to Germany in 1940, so this time we made sure we at least started off with full stomachs. The air was electric as we sat around waiting for the order to move.

It finally came at about 10pm. After a couple of attempts at counting the number of us on parade, we set off. I pulled down my woollen balaclava helmet, and we marched out across the timber yard, on to the pit top. We could hear the noise of the guns growing ever nearer. We passed the pit bath house turning left as we went out of the gates on to the main road in the direction of the city of Gleiwitz. Our route took us past the Russian prisoner-of-war camp. There were signs that they were also preparing to move, and we expected them to be marched in the same direction.

At the head of our column marched the Camp Commandant with a guard. Other guards were spread back along either side of our column at fairly equal distances; but there was no guard at the rear to keep an eye on any stragglers. Twinkle-Toes and One-Eye came with us, but the other guards were old men of the Volkssturm.

The road surface was crisp with hard-packed snow covered by a soft fresh fall. Looking back over our shoulders, we could see the gun flashes reflected off distant snow cover and outlining the houses we were leaving behind.

After a short while we entered the outskirts of Gleiwitz. Outside many of the houses we saw German families preparing to leave their homes. Some were loading small hand-carts with as many of their belongings as they could. Others were loading up small sledges. A few of the men we recognised as miners, and instead of the traditional pit greeting of "gluck auf," we called out to them, "Deutschland kaput." The reply was a stony silence.

In the centre of Gleiwitz we saw much more activity. In one spot a few soldiers helped by a few civilians were erecting barricades behind which we assumed they hoped to hold off the approaching Russians. The road we were marching along led to the railway station, and here our hopes rose as we thought we might be boarding a train to the west. No such luck; we marched right past it.

Through a broken timber in a door at the station, light was streaming across the approach road like a searchlight. The German officer at the head of our party shouted to them to put the light out. His call only prompted one of the station staff to open the door and flood the road with light.

Beyond the station we were forced to leave the main road as more German soldiers were building more barricades using tramcars. We marched along side streets until we had left Gleiwitz behind us, and the coal mine that had caused so much tragedy for many of our friends. As we marched, more snow was falling.

My mind turned back to some of our comrades in the camp who were not with us on this march: such as Bill Burgess, who only a few days ago had joked about 'Uncle Joe's Army' coming to set us free. Now he was dead, killed in that accident just a few days before we left. There had also been cheerful Johnny Waine who delighted us all with his singing of 'The Holy City' at our camp concerts. My thoughts went back further to Mick McClaren, who had defied the Germans by refusing to work. For this he had been sent to a concentration camp. Had he survived? There had also been Taffy Davies, a member of the Royal Monmouthshire Royal Engineers, who, for having been caught by one of the guards with a cartoon of Hitler, had been sent to a local military prison. His sentence was only seven days but we never heard of him again. Many others had been removed from the camp about whose whereabouts no news had ever come back over the grapevine. Some of our coloured comrades had been taken away never to be heard of again. Then there was Sammy from Bethnal Green, who, having crossed Chuck Wilson, was suddenly removed. Rumours led us to believe that he had been denounced as a Jew, thus sealing his fate.

With these thoughts still going through my mind I noticed we were now clear of the town, but along the country roads there was still activity, and there were signs that others had travelled the same way before us. At each crossroads, Germans were awaiting the Russians with tanks or hastily prepared defences. Each group consisted of only a small detachment of soldiers. They looked pitifully inadequate against the advancing Soviet steamroller.

The snow ceased falling and the sky was clearing. The moon shone low in the western sky above the road ahead, which was gradually rising. Walking beside me was one of the elderly Volkssturm guards, almost asleep on his feet. He told me he had been on guard duty all the previous night, and because we had to prepare to move, had not been able to sleep during the day.

Smudger spoke to me, saying it was more than four hours since we had left the camp. "When do you think we will get a stop for a rest?" he wondered. It was as if someone had read his thoughts, for at that moment a call rang out for a halt. We huddled together in small groups. Cigarettes were lit, and to conserve our supplies a single cigarette was passed around each group. Jock felt we should not eat yet as we had dined well before we left the camp, but Smudger had already broken a bar of chocolate into three pieces and gave one to me and the other to Jock. The call then went along the line to get ready to move on; but One-Eye started shouting that we hadn't been counted, so we were made to line up, and the pantomime of counting followed.

While we were being counted, one of the most distressing sights I have ever seen came into view. It was a column of prisoners, obviously from a concentration camp. They looked like walking skeletons; dressed in blue and grey nightgown-type clothes, some with pieces of blankets and others with sacks wrapped around their shoulders; most of them were barefoot. The counting stopped as they slowly went past. I commented to Smudger that they couldn't last very long on the march. Their guards were harassing them as they went past; men and women dressed in the black uniform that I had seen in the prison at Sosnowitz. They stumbled on ahead and finally disappeared over the brow of the hill.

Our guards forgot to finish counting us. Perhaps the sight of those unknown, forgotten shells of human beings made them feel there was no longer any point. There settled over us all, prisoners and guards, an uneasy quiet.

Everyone was becoming increasingly tired and the cold seemed to penetrate right through to the innermost parts of our bodies. The guards, carrying rifles and packs, and wearing very long, heavy overcoats, also seemed to be tiring. A couple of times Twinkle-Toes stumbled and nearly fell over the piles of snow marking the edge of the road, beyond which a sloping field ran down to a river at the bottom of the hill. At last, from the head of the column, a command was shouted to stop and rest. This time we sat even closer together in our little groups and took some food from the stock we carried. Just to one side of the road was a water trough for cattle. Smudger broke the ice, filled two mugs with water and added condensed milk from the Red Cross parcels. The drink was rich and sweet, and it washed down the hard biscuits and cheese that we ate. In order to eat the food I had to raise the lower part of my balaclava, and I realised it was covered with ice where my breath had frozen. I carefully removed the ice, taking care not to damage the wool.

The guards seemed in no hurry to move off. Only after the officer called to them several times did they stand up and start urging us to stand up and fall in line. Once again they went through the farce of counting, but after the third attempt they gave up. We moved on, but before we had gone more than half a mile the pace had slowed down and the older guards seemed to be walking even more slowly than we were.

We took a slippery track to the left, avoiding a town, and found ourselves going uphill again, as the sky began to get lighter. The sound of artillery fire behind us seemed further away now, but when we looked back we could see fires burning in the distance, beyond Gleiwitz to the east.

To our right, in a fold in the rising ground, we passed a few houses with some cattle grouped around some outbuildings. There was no sign of people.

On and on we marched, with tiredness creeping over

us. The loads we were carrying didn't help; but we knew we must not try to make it easier by discarding our tins and packets of food, for they might make the difference between surviving and succumbing. We had waited so long for freedom; we would endure carrying the extra weight.

As daylight spread across the sky we rejoined a road. A short way ahead we saw the crown of the hill. I wondered what lay ahead on the other side. Would there be a place where we might rest for a while?

One-Eye was called to the front of the column, and together with one of the Volkssturm guards was sent ahead while we rested at the top of the hill. We had been moving across the country for about nine hours with only two short breaks, so now many were ready to sleep, and although they were cold, many of my colleagues were closing their eyes. I remembered reading that under these conditions one should never give in to sleep, so I kept moving about on my haunches to keep myself awake. When the two guards who had been sent ahead returned, we were ordered to stand up and start marching again.

The road down the hill twisted and turned, and on one of the bends we saw, lying in the snow at the side of the road, mostly face downwards and in twisted positions, six or seven bodies dressed in the blue and grey striped pyjama uniforms of the skeletal prisoners who had passed us during the night. The snow around their frail bodies was stained with blood. Looking closer, we saw that at least two had had the backs of their heads shot away. The sight filled everyone with disgust and some of the men vomited.

I said to Charlie Wilson: "That's the work of your Nazi friends." He started to reply, but I interrupted, saying I knew his secret and so did some of the others.

He retorted, "The Nazi faith is better than having to give in to rule by Jews and blacks."

Before I could get my hands out of my pockets to punch him, he hurried forward and stood beside one of the guards.

Jock said that until now he had felt that the story that Bill and I had brought back from Sosnowitz was a bit far-fetched; but what Wilson had just said confirmed it. He was indeed a Nazi.

The road levelled out and we had to cross a bridge where there was an army car parked. Standing alongside the car were two German officers wearing very long overcoats and caps trimmed with gold braid. They had broad shoulder pieces which seemed to denote they held some high rank. When the officer from our camp drew level with them he threw a very smart salute and advanced so that he stood directly in front of them. Except for one or two words acknowledging the orders that were given to him, the Camp Commandant remained silent until he was apparently ordered back to look after the prisoners-of-war. The two officers then climbed back into their car together with their driver and drove back along the road we had just covered.

Snow had started to fall again, very lightly. I saw a signpost indicating that the village we were about to enter was called Grunwald. The first few houses appeared to be part of a farm, and then there was a space before the rest of the village came into sight. On the left-hand side of the road, as we rounded a bend, about 40 feet back from a roadside hedge stood a small church, at the side of which was a larger building with a larger door, above which was a big, round window with a stained-glass picture. The centre of the window was dominated by a picture of the Virgin Mary and Child. At the top of the steps, in the partially open doorway, stood a priest in a long dark cloak, with a blue woollen hat on his head. His long, grey hair was blowing about under the edges of the hat. As we marched past, the priest raised his hand making the sign of the cross, then bowed his head, repeating this blessing every few seconds.

I looked back over my shoulder at the church and the priest, and recalled something that had happened in Belgium soon after I had been taken prisoner in 1940. There, a building adjacent to the church had been a convent, and I had handed in a letter which had eventually found its way to my parents in Brighton. After I returned to England, I learned that my parents had had to wait nine months after I had been reported missing in action, before learning that I was alive. Perhaps it was the memory of that church that prompted me to do what I did next; a spontaneous action that might have killed me if it had gone wrong, but which, in the event, may well have saved my life; for as the march westward continued, many prisoners lost their lives from cold, hunger and exhaustion. What we did not know at the time was that our column trudging through that terrible winter was one of many, involving thousands of prisoners-of-war, as well as concentration camp inmates; a phenomenon that was later to become known collectively as the March of Death.

The column stopped moving for some reason. I turned to Smudger and Jock and asked them if they were prepared to take a chance. To my great surprise, despite the fact that back in the camp they had always been plotting something to cause trouble for the Germans or help others who were trying to escape, neither Jock nor Smudger wanted to take a risk now. Jock looked down at the snow and said, "It's your problem. If the Gerry sees you, you might get shot; but if you get away with it, who can say the Russians won't do the same."

"That's probably right, I know, but I could just as easily die on the march," I replied. "This way I can at least enjoy a few days of freedom in the warm again."

After all those years together, we were only able to say short goodbyes. I looked around to see where the guards were situated along the line of the column. Some way back, two of the Volkssturm guards and Twinkle-Toes were carrying someone in uniform into the building where the priest had been standing. We were all standing waiting for the guards to return. When they did, they went straight past us to the front, where the German officer was shouting and gesticulating.

We set off again. The road veered left, then sharply to the right again. We were now out of sight of the guards, who were all at the front. We were about to pass a big yew tree by the side of the road, and running back from the road, a hedge about six feet high. I launched myself full length into the snow under the yew tree. Snow fell from the tree and covered me. The rest of the prisoners marched by and no-one took any notice of the bundle under the tree. When the sound of the marching column had died away, I crawled along the length of the hedge as far from the road as I could. Then, screened by houses and outbuildings, I made my way back towards the road through a garden. Peering around, I saw that the road was still clear; and I ran as fast as my tired legs could manage to the door of the church, and slipped inside. I rested for a moment with my back against the door. Once I had got my puff back, I looked around and saw the priest standing in front of a rough stone font. Smiling, he came towards me and whispered in English, "Welcome, my son." His arm encircled my shoulder and by gentle pressure he moved me from the doorway to a room behind the altar. "I'm glad you came," he said. "Now God will give you sanctuary."

It scarcely seemed possible. I had escaped.

CHAPTER 9

Two nuns came in and together they took me to the other building by way of a passage which linked the church and what seemed to be a hostel. Already lying in two of the beds were colleagues from the mine: Johnnie McNeal of the Argyle and Sutherland Highlanders, and Taffy Thomas, a Welsh Guardsman, whom I knew well from the camp. In civilian life he had been a coal miner in Wales. He was a tall, strong, silent type whose favourite saying was, "The only kind of good German I know of is a dead one."

A third bed was soon made ready and I was bustled into it, uniform, boots and all. A bowl of piping-hot soup was brought in. Warmth, peace of mind for a while, hot soup and a comfortable bed soon brought sleep, but it proved to be a sleep disturbed by a nightmare.

I was sitting alone at a table in a large restaurant. A waiter came over to me. He was Charlie Wilson. He was wearing jackboots and a jacket with tails, but instead of being black, it was German field grey, and had a Union Jack shoulder flash like the ones we had seen in the photograph of the Free Corps traitors. The food he put before me was a bowl of soup and a lump of black bread, just as we had been given in the prison camp. When I had finished the soup he returned to serve the next course, which turned out to be another bowl of soup just the same as the first. He stood near me, gloating. I asked him what he thought he was doing. He laughed and replied that it was more than I deserved for trying to escape and letting my friends help me; that he had told the Commandant, and he had ordered them to be shot; and that this was my final meal before I was shot. I felt his hand on my shoulder and gasped.

Wide-eyed, I looked around. One of the nuns was shaking me by the shoulder, trying to waken me. She had brought a small tray with a mug of coffee. Daylight was shining in through the window. There was hot water for washing in an enamel jug on a table beside my bed. I had not washed properly for a long time. As I stood up, I found I was dressed in a long blue nightgown, although I had climbed into bed in my boots and uniform. We all wondered who had undressed us and put us into the nightgowns, and how they had done it without our noticing. We never found out.

A wash and shave, which removed a considerable growth of beard, made us feel more human. One of the nuns heard Johnnie complaining that his legs were still painful, and saw him looking at the ulcers on his legs. She left the room and returned with another nun, who we found out was the senior among them. She motioned Johnnie to sit on his bed, and then she pulled up his trousers and examined his legs. There was some tutting and whispering, and the young nun left the room. By the time she returned, Johnnie's trousers had been removed and he was lying on the bed. Quietly and without another word they applied some medication to the ulcers. It smelt quite pleasant, even from the other side of the room. Then they applied clean bandages. Without moving him from the bed, they put his trousers back on, and the younger nun, in part English and part German, told him to rest on the bed for a while.

The sun appeared to have passed its zenith when the priest reappeared, followed by a nun we had not previously seen. She carried a tray upon which were some more cups of coffee. Setting the tray on the table she left the room, and the priest motioned us all to join him at the table and drink. There we sat: a German priest, a Welsh miner, a Scottish professional soldier, and me, an English clerk. We learned that the priest's name was Heinrich Olrich. He had persuaded the German soldiers when they had called at his church that there were no escaped prisoners hiding there. He told us we had slept for about 14 hours and said he hoped that we felt well rested. During the night he had heard and seen many columns of prisoners passing through the village. He had received messages that others were hiding in some of the village houses.

The rest of that Wednesday passed quietly and uneventfully. On Thursday morning we were awake when a nun brought us coffee. She apologised that they had not enough food to provide us with a breakfast. We asked her what the situation was regarding food, and she said all they had was some bread and margarine and a little sausage, which the priest had said should be kept for the evening meal. She left us alone for a while, and returned later to collect the cups and tray. Behind her came Father Olrich. He said he was sorry that food was so short, but two army officers had taken nearly all their food only hours before we had arrived. We showed him some of the tins of food we had in our packs. He said he didn't want to take it, but that we could use their stove to cook it if we wished. After some persuasion, he agreed to share a meal made from our supplies with us and the nuns.

Although Johnnie's legs were a little better, we told him to rest while Taffy and I joined the nuns to do the cooking. When we went to light the old stove in the kitchen, we discovered there were no logs, so Father Olrich said he would go and chop them. Taffy wanted to do it for him, but the priest pointed out that the logs were outside and there might still be some German soldiers coming through the village. Reluctantly, Taffy allowed the priest and one of the nuns to go and collect the logs. When the fire was lit, it also supplied hot water and heat for the hostel. In the basement I found some potatoes, and these were soon cleaned and put in a pot to make a stew along with the contents of some of our tins.

We ate the meal, in the company of Father Olrich and three nuns, in the room where we slept. The food was rounded off with cups of hot milk, which we were told came from one of the farmers in the village. The four men then enjoyed a cigarette. The table was cleared and our beds were made ready before it became too dark. There was no chance of lighting lamps, as we heard the Russians were very near.

We had climbed into bed and had the bedclothes pulled up around our chins when the door was opened and there, standing with the priest, were what looked like two Gestapo officers. Father Olrich said, "Yes, they are prisoners-of-war who are too ill to walk, and their commandant has arranged transport for them first thing tomorrow morning."

They accepted what he had said and left without another word. When the priest came back, we thanked him for protecting us. He said he felt sure the transport we wanted would arrive the following day. We all laughed and then settled down for the night. Little did we realise what would happen before the sun rose on Friday morning.

That Thursday night as we settled down in bed, the crunch of the guns seemed to have died down, and I began to wonder if the Russian army was as close as I had thought, or if they were moving in a different direction. Sleep didn't come quite so easily that night, and after a spell of almost total silence from the guns, while I was in that state between being asleep and being awake, a noise like an express train travelling through a tunnel brought me to a full state of awareness. I looked around, and there was a gaping hole in one of the walls, and most of the glass in the windows had been shattered. All three of us quickly pulled on our boots and trousers, scooped up our belongings into our arms, and hurried down to the cellar, almost falling over one another down the stone stairs. The blast from another shell blew the door at the top of the stairs shut behind us. Afterwards we learned that the first shell had entered through the eastern wall, passed straight through our room, and exited through the western wall. Already huddled together in the basement were some of the women and children from the village. The nuns were sitting on an old, broken, box-like object, and Father Olrich moved around trying to calm the young children. With a smile on his face he turned to Johnnie and said he had told the children they were not to be frightened of the Englanders, and that they might be safer if we were with them when the Russians came.

The noise of the heavy gunfire gave way after some time to the staccato sound of machine-gun and rifle fire. It was when this sound was much closer at hand that two German soldiers almost fell down the stairs into the cellar. One had the left sleeve of his overcoat hanging in ribbons and blood streaming down covering his hand. The other was so young and small that he was nearly swallowed up in his uniform, which was much too big for him. Standing there with his rifle by his side I saw it was nearly as tall as him. Tears of fright were running down his cheeks. The older, wounded soldier was carrying an automatic weapon. He turned to the wall, smashed the gun against the brickwork, and threw the remains on to the pile of logs in a basket. He then took the boy's rifle from him and treated it in the same manner. He made to speak to the priest, but before he could say more than two words, Father Olrich told him to sit at the bottom of the stairs with the boy so that they were looking up towards the door. He spoke so fast that I was unable to follow what he was saying, but appeared to be giving him a dressing-down. The boy spoke up and I understood him to say that they had only done as they had been told, because that was the way as Germans they had been brought up by their parents. The older soldier then spoke to me and explained that an officer who had been with them was lying in the hallway, badly wounded. Without waiting to hear any more, two of the nuns went up the stairs. They returned after about five minutes and said they had put the wounded officer in the cupboard near the lavatory.

As the light from the only lamp in the cellar faded, so did the sound of the battle that had been going on above our heads. Now the silence was only broken by the occasional sobbing of the boy soldier. Then we heard the sound of boots on the wooden floor above. The priest rose from the spot where he had been sitting, and walked up the stairs. He had the look of a man going to his execution without knowing how he was to meet his fate. He motioned with his right hand from the top of the steps for no-one to move. He was a little late, as Taffy and I were about half-way up the stairs behind him. There we stayed for a few minutes, and we heard him trying to speak to someone who did not appear to understand him. Then Taffy moved forward to the top of the stairs. I was directly behind him, and I felt Johnnie at my heels. The door that had slammed behind us when the second shell had exploded now hung loosely on one hinge. We saw Father Olrich standing with his hands clasped in front of five soldiers. They were wearing uniforms of a kind we had never seen before. Their helmets had cables hanging from them and their jackets were quilted. The three of us began moving across the rubble to stand beside Father Olrich, but one of the soldiers raised his gun and pointed it at us. We froze, and at this moment a soldier smartly dressed in British uniform came in from outside and he called out something in Russian. I recognised some of the words as meaning "British prisoners-of-war" and "Don't shoot." The gun was lowered and we found ourselves being hugged by the Russians who began talking nineteen to the dozen. The hugging gave way to so much handshaking that my arm felt as though it would fall off. From now on, we were in the care of Uncle Joe Stalin's lads.

The soldier in British uniform now had a chance to introduce himself, and said his name was Sammy (it was probably the Arabic name Sami). He said he had been in a Palestinian Army regiment and then in a German prisoner-of-war camp, although he had been born in the Ukrainian capital, Kiev.

The priest reminded Taffy that there were two German soldiers hiding in the cellar. Sammy overheard him and told the Russian officer, who told Taffy to call down to the people still in the cellar. Pushing the damaged door aside, Taffy shouted down the stairs in his Welsh-accented German, telling everyone to come up to the hall. The first to come through the door was one of the nuns, followed closely by the old ladies from the village, and the children. Then came the other nuns, and after a few moments of waiting, the two rather tatty-looking German soldiers. These two stood side by side in front of the Russian officer with their hands clasped on top of their heads. Stark terror shone from the eyes of the younger soldier and we could see he was trembling with fright and had tears running down his cheeks. The Russian officer spoke to them in good German. He told them the war was now being waged on German soil and the Red Army was making its way to Berlin. He asked them if they were sorry for killing some of his men. The younger one fell to his knees, crying openly, but the older one replied that they had only done their duty, obeying orders. This seemed to please the Russian officer, who said that at least he was a good soldier who obeyed orders, and not one of these snivelling little boys whom Hitler had tried to make into soldiers.

The rest of the Russians stood around with their guns pointing at these miserable-looking Germans. The officer told him that he was unable to take prisoners, and that just as the Germans had dealt with others, so they would be shot. Two of the Russians with light machine-guns slung on their shoulders, knives in their belts, and grenades hanging from their belts, pushed the Germans towards a hole that had been blown in the wall, large enough to walk through. We heard the Russians shouting at their prisoners, and then the officer stood in the hole with his left arm above him grasping the brickwork. After a matter of seconds he dropped his arm to his side. We heard the sharp chatter of the light automatic guns, and the screams of the two Germans. The officer then returned to talk to us. One of the executioners was fastening a watch on to his wrist.

We asked the officer if we could soon move off to somewhere behind the lines. He said he had no idea where we should travel to, as his unit were front-line shock troops, but he warned us we should move about with care, because many of the Russians were trigger-happy and we might easily be shot.

We stood around smoking each others' cigarettes and trying to hold a conversation, but not always understanding what the Russians said. The officer told the priest, "I am sorry I had to shell your church but the German soldiers had fought from behind the doors of the building and I had to try and beat them. Thank you for looking after our allies and protecting them. Soon I will be leaving." Father Olrich replied that he understood that the damage was a misfortune of war.

During all this, the wounded German officer whom the nuns had hidden in a cupboard near the lavatory had remained undiscovered.

Now the Russian shock-troops moved towards the opening that had been the doorway and signalled for us to follow. I asked if we should first collect our belongings. The officer told us to hurry up and left two of his men to escort us. While we were in our bedroom fetching our possessions, we heard some activity in the hall. We looked out of the window and saw one of the soldiers dragging the wounded German officer by his arms, which were obviously already broken. Blood had dried on the front of his tunic, and part of the side of his face had been shot away. By the look in his eyes, he knew that the Russians were going to shoot him in cold blood. They dragged him down on to the road, propped him up against a tree, and shot him in the chest and head. As he toppled over, his blood spurted on to the snow.

When we were ready, the two Russian soldiers who had been left as our guides escorted us out of the village, back in the direction from which we had arrived. We continued to walk with them to the farm that we had seen just before we had entered the village in our marching column. In one of the farm houses, the Russian advance party had set up their headquarters. Here we met a very smartly dressed Russian officer who stood over six feet tall, and introduced himself in English.

We told him of our various journeys from the camps. He apologised for not being able to offer us a cigarette, saying he was a non-smoker; but he insisted that we take a drink with him. He took an army water bottle from the desk by his side and poured for each of us in turn a drink into the cup which fitted on its neck. When it came to my turn, I followed suit with the others, and drank it in one. I felt it running down inside me, at first warming my throat and stomach; and then I felt the full heat of the powerful liquid. It was my first taste of vodka.

The only food he was able to offer us was in the form of sweets. There was a large box of these on one of the smaller tables in the room. We were pleased to eat them, as they took away the burning sensation caused by the vodka. We spoke for some while of our escapades, until his presence was required elsewhere by some of the tank commanders. We suggested that it would be safer for us to move back behind the lines before the night came again. He told us we would have to travel on foot, but he would provide us with instructions and a map. He said that the Russians had set up an organisation to help any British prisoners-of-war that were found, and that we should proceed to Czestochowa, a Polish city about 60 miles northeast of Gleiwitz.

With a firm handshake and an embrace, he bade us farewell and hoped that we would soon be home in England. The two soldiers, our escorts, were called, and we started to retrace our footsteps along the way we had come the previous Monday night and Tuesday morning. Thus began my long journey towards freedom; but in order to reach my home in the west, I would first have to make a long, zig-zag journey much further eastwards than I had ever dreamed the war would take me; eventually into the Soviet Union.

CHAPTER 10

There was now more spring in our steps, as we felt we were at last free, even though we were no nearer home in mileage than we had been before the Russians had arrived. We made good progress and passed many Russian soldiers heading west. Some of them called out that they were on their way to Berlin. Just before dusk we saw a company of horsemen coming towards us, and our escorts stopped and spoke to them. Afterwards they explained that the horsemen were Cossacks, and that their jobs were rounding up stray Germans and maintaining liaison with the front line. As night approached, we all felt that at the next house or farm we should stop for the night. Soon we saw some farm buildings to our left.

Sammy, Johnnie, Taffy and I walked across the yard to the front door of the first house. I banged on the door and heard someone moving about, but nobody came to open up. Standing slightly to one side, I kicked the door, and it opened. Inside stood a group of women, huddled together, and a very small boy. I told them we were escaped British prisoners and we intended to spend the night in their house.

The two Russian soldiers were by this time nowhere to be seen. In the morning we learned that they had gone to the back of the farm and found a chicken house. There they made themselves a supper of boiled chicken and then went to sleep in the hen-house.

Inside the farm-house we found some older people. They were the parents of the women who had been behind the door when we opened it. They told us that the previous night, when they realised the Russians were coming, they had hidden in the cow-shed. They had watched the Russians go by through cracks between badly-placed boards, and they had hidden in the piles of fodder.

It was now dark, so the very heavy curtains were drawn across the windows and the kitchen was illuminated by three old-fashioned oil lamps. We told the German who appeared to be the farmer that we needed something to eat. There was a general bustling about and wood was fed into the range. Potatoes were brought up from a storage space under the floor, and eggs were brought out of the larder. We sat down to a table with a white cloth and very large plates piled with eggs and chips. This was the first time I had tasted eggs and chips since we had left France to enter Belgium in 1940. It was followed by big pieces of home-made apple pie and pots of home-brewed beer. It was wonderful.

Although it was quite early evening, we were full and tired. The young woman sensed that we wanted to go to sleep, so she told the boy to fetch some light. Each of us was given a candle to carry, and she showed us upstairs to a room which seemed to occupy the whole of the upper storey. There were six beds. I asked her if these were the family's beds, but she only shook her head. After she left, we carefully stowed our packs and boots, then undressed with hardly a word being spoken and climbed into a bed each, leaving two beds free.

After a long night's uninterrupted sleep, I found myself lying in that happy state of being neither asleep nor quite awake. The sun had risen and moved around just enough for its rays to strike a mirror and reflect straight into my eyes. The brightness was almost painful even through my closed eyelids. I turned my head to one side, and saw that Sammy was just beginning to stir. Then I noticed the older two Germans asleep in one of the two other beds, and the woman and her boy in the other. Outside we could hear cattle milling around and jangling chains by which they were tethered to a fence.

Sammy, Taffy, Johnnie and I got up and started to dress. The older Germans rose out of their bed. They had slept in the clothes we had seen them in downstairs. The boy was moving, awakened by our noises. He had on a long nightshirt which almost enveloped him. His mother was similarly dressed, but on her head she still had the scarf which had been there when we had seen her crouching behind the door.

The parents took the boy down the stairway with them as we were dressing and stamping on our boots. The young woman, whose name was Frieda, called out good morning to us and said that there would be some coffee in the kitchen for us. At the far corner of the room stood a large bowl and a jug of water, which we used to wash ourselves, then we went down for a cup of coffee; after which, collecting our belongings together, we found our Russian escorts preparing breakfast with eggs they had collected from the hen-house and bread they had found hidden away in the roof of the barn. The fat they used for frying, I learned later, had been found in a large rusty bucket hanging on the wall. They told us about their chicken supper. For a further drink, we opened another tin of condensed milk and mixed it with water that had been heated over the fire they had lit in the middle of the barn floor.

Inwardly fortified, we set out on the next part of our journey. The morning passed slowly and uneventfully. Taffy and I thought it would be a good idea to return to the camp and stock up from the Red Cross parcels that had been left behind. As we drew near to Gleiwitz again, we heard the rumble of artillery fire. A Russian driving a car told us that German soldiers and tanks were putting up resistance in the city centre area, and we would have to make a detour. Just as we were approaching the place where we had left Gleiwitz under German guards on the Monday, we were diverted and had to head back into the countryside and to skirt around the town. That put paid to going back to the camp for food.

It was late January and dusk would fall early, so we again needed to find somewhere to spend the night under cover and in safety. I remembered having passed a large building that looked like a school or office block about two kilometres east of Gleiwitz when I had been taken for examination at a hospital before being diagnosed as having stone dust in my lungs. I told the Russians about the building and they studied the map and located it near a place called Laband. Taffy recalled that one of the civilians in the mine had told him there had been another prisoner-of-war camp there and a mining college nearby.

It was fairly near, so we quickened our pace. After passing a broken signpost showing the distance to Laband we saw a large building standing a little way back from the road behind a brick wall. The wall was badly damaged by shellfire and the large pillars at the entrance were almost completely demolished. At the entrance to the building there were many bodies of German soldiers, and we had to move aside one that was blocking the doorway.

Off the entrance hall were a number of large rooms which we could see by the manner of their furnishings were either lecture rooms or classrooms. A doorway near the bottom of a heavy, carved wooden staircase led into a dining-room with dark wood refectory tables, and leading off that was a kitchen where we found a stove still burning, supplying heating for the whole building. The light fittings were all broken, but we found the ends of some candles, and lit them. We searched the kitchen and other ground-floor rooms, and found more candles and some oil lamps. In the larder we found some lightly cured sliced pork, similar to bacon. We noticed that an electric switch was in the 'on' position, and a hotplate in the kitchen was glowing, so although there was no electric light, we would be able to use the stove and hotplate. Soon two of us were organising the cooking while three went upstairs to explore the other floors. They returned after a while to tell us there were bedrooms and stock cupboards with new clothes stored in them. After supper we took advantage of the hot water that was available, to thoroughly wash and shave. The Russians had no razors. Not to be outdone, they chose a crescent-shaped shard from the broken glass of a book-case, and used it to remove several days' growth of beard. With their whiskers gone and their faces washed, they looked much younger.

Sitting around the table in the kitchen with a hot drink, we talked, and having spent two days with the Russians and having Sammy with us, we found we could have a conversation even if it was only limited. The older of our escorts was 21 and the younger 19. They came from the far east of Russia and had worked on the railway until a few months earlier. Then they had been called up into the army because heavy losses had been incurred on the front.

Once more we were all tired, so taking our candles and lamps with us, we went upstairs to the bedrooms. The beds were marvellous; we had slept in nothing like them for many years: thick feather mattresses, heavy white sheets and colourful bedspreads. We raided the linen cupboards and found clean shirts and pullovers. This enabled us to discard the dirty old ones we had on.

Our Russian friends decided that they would sleep on the landing outside our rooms, and curled up there in blankets. This proved to be a blessing, for in the early hours of the morning some rampaging Russian soldiers burst into the school and started smashing up whatever had not already been broken. The older Russian with us, whose name was Ivan, shouted down to them and fired a few shots from his rifle over their heads. Calling them cookhouse soldiers and not fighting men, he soon had them running out of the door into the snow. We went downstairs and discovered that the hooligans had started a fire on the floor in the dining-room. It was put out using a fire bucket of sand and a heavy fire blanket.

Early next morning the younger of the two Russians, whose name we never found out, told Sammy that he had found some food for breakfast. A saucepan of coffee had been made and stood on the hob. Cleaning up, we assembled our packs and went back to the kitchen. There was a large, square cherry cake which Ivan cut into chunky slices. We washed it down with strong coffee, and then set off again. Before long we had a stroke of luck, managing to thumb a lift in a Russian military car, which took us most of the way.

Early in the afternoon, we arrived in the cathedral city of Czestokowa.

CHAPTER 11

The driver knew we should have to report to the Russian military police at a headquarters they had set up in the Town Hall in the city centre, so he took us there. We went in and were taken to the officer-in-charge; a short, tubby woman. Sammy speeded things up for us by talking with her in fluent Russian; she wrote down our details, and allocated us billets, agreeing to let Johnnie, Sammy, Taffy and me stay together. Two other military policewomen drove us to a big old house in a neighbourhood where all the other buildings were blocks of flats.

One of the policewomen banged on the door with the butt of her pistol. After the noise of bolts being drawn back, a frightened-looking, balding man opened the door. The policewoman told him sharply that he was responsible for our well-being and was to find us beds and food until arrangements had been made to move us for our journey home. That last bit sounded very good.

In the living-room he introduced us to his wife and daughter. Our host's name was Peter and his wife was called Stephanie. Peter was a lot older than Stephanie, who was in her mid-30s. The girl was about 12, but Peter told me he was not the girl's father. As we sat around in what at first seemed a strained atmosphere, Peter explained that he had been in a cavalry regiment when the Germans had invaded Poland. In the first few days of the war, their troop had been overrun and he found he was the sole survivor. He had hidden in a wooden shed near the railway line at Breslau, a major city which is now in Poland and called Wroclaw. He had changed out of his uniform into some civilian clothes that he found in the shed, in a pocket of which he found some papers which indicated that the clothes belonged to one Peter Gertwitch. He took on that identity, resolving never again to use his real name.

We spent the first full day with our new hosts helping in the house, tidying up our clothes, and taking stock of what personal belongings we had left. I was surprised that the family had such good stocks of food, out of which they prepared two meals a day. Early morning breakfast consisted of dried cereal and hot milk followed by uncooked smoked fish with bread, or grilled slices of bacon, and thick, well-buttered slices of home-made bread. There was a choice of drink. I took coffee, Sammy had a chocolate drink, and the others chose peppermint tea.

Our hosts appeared to be worried that we might have to hang around for a long time. We knew there might be a long wait but it should not have an effect on their supplies as the Russians brought enough food each day to feed an extra eight, and we were only four more.

That night in bed, Johnnie said he had a feeling the Gertwitch family were up to something. In the back of a cupboard off the kitchen, he had seen some cases already labelled for an address in Warsaw. When Stephanie had seen him looking at them, she had said her husband had kept them packed for some years in case they needed to leave while the Germans had been there; but Johnnie said the labels looked as if they had been written very recently.

Two mornings later, we awoke to find that our hosts had vanished, along with the suitcases and most of the supplies from the kitchen. Late in the afternoon two Russian women soldiers brought some food as usual, and asked what had become of the Poles who had been looking after us. We told them what had happened. They told Sammy we should have informed the officer in charge of the military police earlier; however, as it was getting late, we were to stay in the house another night and report in the morning.

Not knowing what would happen in the morning, we spent a troubled night. To put on a good show, we presented ourselves early at the police depot, where the tubby Russian policewoman was waiting for us. We told her the story to the best of our ability, and then she sat back in her chair and invited us to sit down. She pointed out that there was a curfew on the movements of civilians in order to control known collaborators and some Germans who were trying to pass themselves off as Poles. They had been suspicious of the Gertwitch family, as according to the town records there should have been older people in the house. I told her the story that he had related about changing his name. She said the Russian authorities would make enquiries in Warsaw, because of the labels on the cases. If she wanted any more help, she would send for us. In the meantime, we would be sent to live with another family who were known to be true Poles.

We were now taken with our packs in a lorry along the main road toward the Cathedral of the Black Madonna, which dominated the town. The lorry stopped near the entrance to a high block of flats. We passed through a doorway into a courtyard, and then up some stairs, to a flat on the second floor, where we were introduced to another family, who welcomed us to their home. The man spoke reasonable English, and after the policewoman left he introduced us to the rest of the household. After explaining that he had been a colonel in the Polish army, and with the fall of Poland he had for two years been interned by the Germans, he said his name was Jan and his wife's was Anna. He then called in another woman aged about 25, and introduced her as their unmarried daughter, Maria. He told his wife to bring in a bottle of schnapps and some glasses, and we sat around convivially, some on chairs and some on the floor, drinking and relating our various experiences as prisoners of the Germans. When he had first been interned, the Germans had forced Jan to work on a farm, even though by profession he was a doctor of medicine, specialising in orthopaedics.

Anna seemed happy to have Englishmen in the house, and after a while suggested we might like to clean ourselves up before eating the main meal of the day. A small sitting-room was set aside for our use, where we were each given some drawer-space. After a few moments she returned and told us that, if we wished, we could use the bathroom next-door to the sitting-room and have a shower. This was too good an opportunity to miss, so we took turns, and it was four very clean soldiers who presented themselves to the family when we were called for dinner. Following the wife and daughter's example, we stood behind our chairs until Jan had said a lengthy grace. Afterwards Johnnie offered to help clear the table, but Jan told him the women would to see to that, and he should sit down and relax.

Maria, the daughter, returned bearing a large tray on which stood two coffee pots, cups, and a small bottle of brandy. We drank hot coffee laced with brandy, slumped down into comfortable cushions, and looked at family photos produced from a drawer. All this cosy domesticity felt a long way away from the camp, and from the horrors we had so recently seen along the roads west of Gleiwitz.

During our conversation, Jan said that Maria worked every other day during the daytime in a soldiers' canteen and had heard from some of the Russians that there were some British planes at Warsaw. Perhaps, he said, they had come to take us home.

Jan said Maria had a gift for foretelling future events and would be pleased to do so for us. We were all rather sceptical, but agreed to have our fortunes told. However, she said she could only do it while sitting on a particular seat on the steps leading up to the cathedral. After some persuasion by her mother, she agreed to do so that evening.

On the cathedral steps, we were each told that we had a girlfriend waiting for us in England, and that soon after returning home we would be married. As far as I know this was only true in my case, as Taffy and Johnnie were already married, while Sammy wasn't even from England. He had told us he wanted to go to Palestine.

When we got back to the flat, we produced tins of drinking-chocolate from our packs, and before we went to bed, Anna made us each a big mug of hot chocolate.

The next day we visited the canteen where Maria worked, and there we met two Russians who said they would drive us to Warsaw in their lorry the following day, a distance of 130 miles. We gave them five cigarettes, which was all we had to offer.

The following day we met the Russians as arranged, but even though they drove very fast, the whole plan was doomed. After about an hour on the road, the lorry was stopped and we were ordered out by two other Russians with machine-guns. They said the planes were not for us and had already returned to England. The lorry was allowed to travel on and we had to wait at the camp where we had been halted while they prepared another lorry to take us back. That evening we were very gloomy and wondered if the Russians were going to hold us for a long time, or even if they were going to let us go home at all.

Just after midnight there was a terrific banging on the door of the flat and Jan went to see who it was. We found our woman police officer standing there, and she told us to be ready to move off in half-an-hour. Hurriedly we packed and bade farewell to our hosts. There were tears and kisses as we said goodbye, and off we went in a comfortable car, heading out of Czestochowa on the road towards Krakow, 60 miles to the southeast.

The driver was clearly finding the drive difficult in the pitch darkness, and kept bumping into things, although nothing serious happened; and eventually he decided to stop and wait until daylight. He knocked on the next door he came to, and after some shouting it was opened by two young women dressed in farm-workers' clothes. The driver talked with them in Russian, and the only words I understood were "English prisoners-of-war". Finally he beckoned to us to get out of the car and go into the house.

On the ground floor there were two rooms: one very small, housing a tap over a wooden sink and a wood-fired boiler, which was lit; the other, larger, containing an oven with a curved top, above which was a contraption made of iron pipes, wire and animal skins. This, we were told, was a bed for whoever had to start work first in the morning, so that the heat from the oven helped them get a good night's sleep.

The amount of noise we were making had awoken the rest of the household, and an interior door opened, revealing a stairway, where some more women were now standing. It turned out that, in all, six women lived in the house. The two who had let us in now told the others to take us upstairs and make room for us to go to bed. The Russian driver stayed downstairs.

The upper storey was all one room, containing two old brass bedsteads side-by-side against a wall. The bed linen on them appeared clean and fresh, while the rest of the room looked like a fur trapper's store. Animal skins lay all over the place, some rolled up like bolsters. The only light came from a lamp which smelt as though it was burning animal fat. The women told us we were to use the beds, which were kept for visitors.

Once we were in bed and the women had settled down among the furs, they started to talk to us, and by signs and a mixture of German and Polish, we were able to tell them of our adventures. One whose name was Kala told us she had hidden two prisoners from a concentration camp in a small barn at the back of the house. One was a dumb man, the other a young Jewish woman. Sleep finally came, but all too soon we were awakened, as the Russian driver was getting ready to move on. The women told him there were two other escaped prisoners who might want to travel with us, and he agreed to take them if they wanted to come.

Kala fetched the two who had been hiding in the barn. After they had been given coffee and hot bread rolls, the woman said they wanted to travel to Palestine. The man was unable to speak as his throat had been damaged in the concentration camp.

We all climbed into the car and set off for Krakow. When we got there, the car stopped near a railway station. We had arrived in Poland's historic former capital, and now its second city.

CHAPTER 12

When we got out of the car on arrival in Krakow we were directed to a large building about five storeys high on the opposite side of the road, guarded by two smart Russian soldiers. They both shook our hands and one of them escorted us inside, where we were met by two women soldiers who asked us from which camps we had come. We told them, adding that the man and woman who had been hiding in the barn had come from the same area as Taffy, Johnnie and myself.

The building had obviously been a major hotel in peacetime, but for now it was being used to house escaped prisoners-of-war. We were allocated a room on the first floor containing a double bed, two sofas and a table and chairs, which we repositioned near the window so that we could look out while sitting at it. Eventually some Poles who worked in the building brought us a meal, and told us we were in what had once been the best hotel in Krakow. We sat down to eat and enjoy the luxury while we could.

As darkness fell, we were told to close the shutters at the windows and pull the curtains to conserve heat. The electric lights were working, so we switched them on and made ourselves very comfortable. The camp now seemed a long way away, although it was only 60 miles to the west. We had travelled more or less along two sides of an equilateral triangle, up from Gleiwitz to Czestochowa, then down from Czestochowa to Krakow. What we did not know at the time was that if we had come by the direct route from Gleiwitz to Krakow, we would have passed the most notorious death camp of the Second World War – Auschwitz.

We exchanged stories with the Jewish couple. The man had been taken to a concentration camp at Lodz in central Poland, where he was forced to help the Germans to prepare other Jews for 'processing'. A few days before the camp had been closed he had learned that he was going to be sent to the gas chambers as well, but a Pole had smuggled him out of the camp hidden under a load of clothes taken from Jews who had just been gassed. Once away from the camp, he had run until he could run no more, and then had hidden in a clamp of root vegetables. (Editor's note: there is no indication in the manuscript of how the dumb man told his story. One can only conjecture that perhaps he wrote it.)

The young woman told us her name was Hannah, and that she had been taken from Warsaw with her parents to another concentration camp, where her father, who had been a vet, was forced to extract the gold teeth from dead Jews. Her job had been to help her father and present a record of work each day to the officer in charge. Her life had been spared because she worked with her father and because the officer wanted sex with her.

When the Russian army was approaching, those of the survivors in her camp who could walk had clubbed to death two guards at the gate and fled under cover of night. Many were so weak that they fell by the wayside as the group walked across the countryside, not knowing where they were going, but Hannah and her father had managed to keep moving; until the following night he had succumbed to the cold, and Hannah was left on her own. That was when she had been found by the Polish women at the house, who hid her in the barn. The next morning, the dumb man had turned up there as well.

Gradually the truth about life in the concentration camps was unfolded to us. Until now they had only been stories that we had heard from people who knew someone else who had seen them from a distance. Hannah showed us the number she had been given at the concentration camp burnt on her forearm and tattooed across her left breast. The dumb man had been similarly treated. He looked about half his normal weight, and Hannah was little more than a bundle of bones.

Next morning we were told we were free to go into the town if we wished, but to be sure and leave someone in the rooms to guard our possessions. Neither of our two Jewish friends wanted to leave the hotel, and Taffy said he would stay and keep them company for part of the day. So Johnnie and I went for a walk together, and Sammy decided to go off on his own to see if he could find anyone he knew. We soon realised that we were far from being the only escaped prisoners in Krakow.

We visited the station and the market place, then the entrance to the old walled city and what appeared to be a keep. The walls around the old city were very thick, and just inside the entrance was a stone stairway leading to the top. We asked a Russian soldier walking among stalls where all sorts of goods were on sale whether we could walk around the top of the wall. He said he hadn't been told it was out of bounds, and he had seen other Russians walking along the wall near the prison. So we then decided that we would explore the city from the top of the wall, and our new Russian chum said he would come with us and look after us. We were pleased to have his company.

Walking along the top, we looked down to inner parts of the old city, and saw a multiplicity of market stalls selling black market goods and produce from the countryside.

And then we got another surprise. At the far side of the wall we looked down into the yard of the prison, and saw a few soldiers dressed in very shabby German uniforms. Looking closer, we saw that they all had Union Jack flashes sewn on their sleeves, with the words Free Corps above them in English and German – just like the uniforms I had seen in those photographs at Sosnowitz.

Back at the hotel, a woman soldier told us to go down to the dining-room, where we would hear something we had all been waiting for.

Leaving our two Jewish friends in the room, we assembled with a few hundred other ex-prisoners downstairs, and a British officer stood up and told us that the following morning we would be put on a train and taken to Odessa, a Ukrainian port on the Black Sea coast, and there we would be put on a British ship to sail home.

The room resounded to our cheers, and perhaps a few tears. Then the officer walked among us talking to us in groups, reassuring us that we would soon be home, and that once on board a British ship, we could send messages to our loved-ones.

Johnnie asked him about the Free Corps men, and he replied that they would be treated in the same way as other German prisoners-of-war, and that their fate would depend on their Russian captors.

I spent my 25th birthday in a camp in Odessa, having my clothes deloused and taking a bath. The bath-house was mixed, and the Russian women soldiers laughed when we tried to cover up our naked bodies as they passed among us.

Two days later we set sail for England. There are no words to describe my feelings as the Ukrainian coastline receded astern. I had lost five years of my life and three stone in weight. But I had fought my underground war to the best of my ability, and had made a mockery of the words of that cocky German officer in Ypres who had declared, "Tommy, for you the war is over."

Ahead lay home, my sweetheart, my parents, and peace. In August, 1945, Edith and I were married in St Peter's Old Church, Preston Park, Brighton. In February, 1947, our son, Albert John was born. When he grew up and went to university, he studied Russian.

THE END

EDITOR'S NOTE

My late father left me the manuscript on which this book is based. He died of cancer in Brighton in September 1984. I had always felt proud of what Dad did in the War; but it was not until later in life that I truly appreciated what a nightmare that experience must have been. I have not altered any of the substance; I have merely improved the literary presentation for clarity and ease of reading, and added some minor elements of background and geography, plus some short linking paragraphs to help the story flow. The yarn itself is totally Dad's, not mine. I have changed some names because, even if these men were still alive 70 years after the war, it would be extremely difficult to find them. Reading and editing this material has been a humbling process; one that makes me salute my father, and all his comrades, for their incredible bravery and fortitude.

* * * * *

FICTION BY ALBERT JOHN CLACK

AVAILABLE FROM AMAZON

Murder at the Theatre Royal

When Hamlet drags the body of Polonius on to the stage, Sir Roger Nutley, the famous actor playing him, is really dead. Two years ago, a court failed to convict Sir Roger of sex offences. But he has other dark secrets: a cocaine habit, high-class prostitutes, and gangland connections.

Murder of a British Patriot

While campaigning for Britain to leave the European Union in the June 2016 referendum, George Marshall, leader of the British Patriotic Party, is shot dead. Suspects include a Muslim student, a far-right political rival, a left-wing activist, and three older people with a grudge from the 1984 miners' strike.